The Profit Blueprint

Strategies for Reducing Costs, Enhancing Efficiency, and Boosting Your Bottom Line

CES Cost Saving Institute

CBW Publishing

2025

978-0-9823158-9-7

Table of Contents

Introduction

In the fiercely competitive landscape of modern business, the difference between thriving and barely surviving often comes down to one crucial factor: how well you manage your costs. A recent study by McKinsey & Company found that companies that excel at cost management are 40% more likely to outperform their peers. Let that sink in for a moment.

Whether you're a financial manager looking to optimize your budget, a C-suite executive aiming to boost profitability, an operations manager streamlining your supply chain, or an entrepreneur trying to scale your business, this book is for you. I've designed "The Profit Blueprint" to be a practical, hands-on guide that will help you reduce costs, enhance efficiency, and ultimately, boost your bottom line.

At its core, this book is built on a simple but powerful idea: strategic cost management is the key to sustainable business growth and staying ahead of the competition. Throughout these pages, we'll dive into the nitty-gritty of how to identify cost-saving opportunities, implement effective expense management systems, and create a culture of continuous improvement.

We'll start by laying a solid foundation, exploring the fundamental principles of cost management and why it matters now more than ever. From there, we'll move into more advanced topics, such as optimizing your supply chain, leveraging technology for efficiency, and developing a long-term cost strategy. Each chapter builds upon the last, giving you a comprehensive roadmap to transforming your business.

But this isn't just another dry business book filled with abstract theories. "The Profit Blueprint" is packed with real-world case studies, practical exercises, and actionable advice that you can start applying today. I've also tapped into my network of industry experts to bring you fresh insights and cutting-edge strategies that you won't find anywhere else.

So here's my challenge to you: don't just read this book – use it. Take the strategies and techniques you learn here and put them into practice in your own business. Whether you're looking to trim a few percentage points off your operating costs or completely overhaul your financial strategy, the tools you need are within these pages.

In the end, mastering cost management is about more than just boosting profits – it's about building a sustainable, thriving business that can weather any storm. So let's roll up our sleeves and get started on this journey together. With "The Profit Blueprint" as your guide, you'll be well on your way to achieving your business goals and securing your financial future.

Chapter 1: Foundations of Cost Management

Have you ever wondered why some businesses thrive while others struggle to keep their doors open? It's often not because one has a better product or a more talented team but because one has a tighter grip on their costs. Consider a bustling coffee shop that you pass by every morning. On the surface, it seems like any other, but delve a little deeper, and you might find a meticulous owner who knows the cost of every coffee bean, cup, and employee hour. It's this kind of detailed cost management that sets successful businesses apart. In this chapter, we'll uncover the building blocks of cost management, offering you insights into where your money goes and how to control it effectively.

1.1 Understanding Cost Structures in Business

Cost structures are the backbone of your financial strategy, dictating how expenses are categorized and managed within your organization. At the heart of any cost structure, you'll find two primary components: fixed costs and variable costs. Fixed costs, like rent or salaries, remain constant regardless of your production output. They are the unwavering expenses you must cover month after month. On the other hand, variable costs fluctuate with production activity, including materials and commissions. Understanding these costs helps you maintain financial stability by allowing you to predict and manage your cash flow more effectively, ensuring you can meet your financial obligations even when business fluctuates. For instance, in a busy manufacturing plant, fixed costs might include the lease of a factory building, while variable costs could be the raw materials needed for production. Balance these costs wisely, and you're on your way to a more predictable financial future.

When you look across industries, you'll notice how cost structures differ dramatically. A manufacturing company, for example, will have substantial fixed costs tied up in machinery and facilities, whereas a service-oriented business might find its costs tied more to labor and customer acquisition. Retail businesses often operate on thin margins, requiring close attention to both fixed and variable costs. In the service industry, costs can be more fluid, with labor playing a significant role in the overall cost structure. Recognizing these differences is critical, as it informs how you approach cost management and pricing strategies within your respective industry.

Cost behavior analysis examines how costs evolve with changes in business activity, offering key insights into the dynamics of your financial landscape. Economies of scale come into play when increased production leads to lower per-unit costs, enhancing your competitive edge. Conversely, understanding your break-even point—the stage where total costs match total revenue—guides you in setting realistic and profitable pricing strategies. This analysis is essential for navigating the complexities of production scales, ensuring that you maximize profitability while minimizing unnecessary expenses. By mastering these concepts, you gain the ability to fine-tune your operations and make informed financial decisions that drive sustainable growth.

The impact of your cost structure on pricing strategy cannot be overstated. Cost-plus pricing, where a fixed percentage is added to costs to set prices, ensures you cover expenses and earn a profit. However, this method might not always align with what the market is willing to pay. In contrast, value-based pricing allows you to set higher prices if customers perceive your product as superior. Take Apple Inc., for example. They've mastered the art of value-based pricing, charging a premium for their innovative products because customers see the value in their brand. Understanding your cost structure and how it influences pricing decisions is crucial for crafting a strategy that maximizes profitability while staying competitive in the marketplace. By aligning your pricing with your costs and customer perceptions, you can position your business for success.

Visual Element: Cost Structure Diagram

To help you visualize these concepts, here's a simple diagram breaking down fixed costs, variable costs, and their role in pricing strategies. You can use this to map your own business expenses and identify areas for improvement. Take a moment to reflect on how your current cost structure aligns with your pricing strategy. Consider whether adjustments are needed to optimize costs and enhance profitability.

1.2 Identifying Hidden Costs That Impact Profitability

In the bustling world of business, hidden costs can quietly chip away at profitability, much like termites gnawing at the foundation of a house. These unnoticed expenses can catch even the savviest of managers off guard. Take the supply chain, for instance. On the surface, it might seem like a well-oiled machine, delivering goods just in time and keeping shelves stocked. But delve a little deeper, and you might uncover inefficiencies that, over time, inflate costs significantly. Inefficiencies in routing, warehousing, or even supplier relationships can silently drain resources. Then there's the matter of overlooked maintenance costs. Equipment that breaks down unexpectedly can halt production, leading to costly downtime and repairs that could have been avoided with regular preventive maintenance. And let's not forget employee turnover costs, which can sneak up on you, manifesting as recruitment fees, training new hires, and lost productivity. These hidden costs, if left unmanaged, have a profound impact on your bottom line.

The financial health of a company relies heavily on its ability to identify and control these hidden costs. When unaccounted for, they can slowly erode net profit margins, making it harder to achieve long-term financial sustainability. Imagine running a marathon with a pebble in your shoe. You might not notice it at first, but over time, it becomes a significant hindrance. Similarly, hidden costs might start small but can accumulate, reducing profitability and putting pressure on cash flow. This erosion can make it challenging to reinvest in growth opportunities or weather economic downturns. The implications are clear: to maintain fiscal health, these costs must be brought to light and addressed.

Detecting hidden costs requires a keen eye and a proactive approach. One effective method is conducting regular process audits. By systematically reviewing operations, you can identify inefficiencies and areas where resources may be wasted. Cost variance analysis is another powerful tool, allowing you to compare expected costs against actual expenditures, highlighting discrepancies that might indicate hidden costs. Technology also plays a crucial role in cost tracking. Modern software solutions can provide real-time insights into spending patterns and flag anomalies that warrant further investigation. These tools, combined with a diligent approach, help shine a light on hidden costs lurking in the shadows of your operation.

Once identified, the next step is to mitigate these hidden costs. Streamlining processes is a straightforward yet effective strategy. By optimizing workflows and eliminating redundancies, you can reduce waste and improve efficiency. Implementing preventive maintenance programs is another strategy that pays dividends. Regular upkeep of equipment not only extends its lifespan but also prevents costly breakdowns and production delays. Enhancing employee retention strategies can significantly reduce turnover costs. Providing competitive compensation, fostering a positive work environment, and offering growth opportunities encourage employees to stay, reducing the need for constant recruitment and training. These strategies, while seemingly simple, can have a profound impact on your operational efficiency and overall financial health.

Textual Element: Case Study - A Manufacturing Company's Hidden Costs

Consider a large manufacturing company that was struggling with profitability despite robust sales figures. Through a detailed process audit, they discovered inefficiencies in their supply chain, particularly in how raw materials were sourced and stored. By renegotiating supplier contracts and optimizing inventory levels, they managed to save significant costs. Simultaneously, they implemented a preventive maintenance program, reducing equipment downtime by 30%. Finally, by addressing employee satisfaction through better engagement and career development opportunities, they saw a 25% decrease in turnover rates. This case illustrates the tangible benefits of identifying and addressing hidden costs, offering a clear path to enhanced profitability.

By recognizing these hidden costs and taking decisive action, businesses can safeguard their profit margins and ensure sustainable success. Whether it's through audits, employing advanced technology, or enhancing employee engagement, addressing these hidden costs can lead to significant improvements in financial performance. Understanding and tackling these sneaky expenses is more than just good housekeeping; it's a vital part of running a profitable and resilient business.

1.3 The Importance of Financial Planning in Cost Reduction

In the world of business, effective financial planning serves as your strategic playbook for managing costs and ensuring long-term success. You wouldn't embark on a road trip without a map, and similarly, you shouldn't navigate the complexities of business without a well-crafted financial plan. At the core of this planning is the integration of budgeting and forecasting. Budgeting lays out your financial expectations for a period, providing a clear picture of where resources will be allocated. Forecasting, on the other hand, offers a dynamic view, predicting future financial conditions based on past performance and current trends. Together, they form a powerful duo, enabling you to anticipate challenges and seize opportunities, steering your business toward profitability. It's about setting a financial course that aligns with your strategic goals, ensuring you have the resources to support growth while avoiding unnecessary expenditures.

Scenario planning adds another layer of depth to financial planning, preparing you for the unexpected twists and turns that business can throw your way. By exploring various scenarios, from best-case to worst-case, you gain a robust understanding of potential risks and rewards. This proactive approach allows you to develop contingency plans, ensuring you're not caught off guard by market shifts or economic downturns. When integrated with your business strategy, financial planning becomes more than just a numbers game. It aligns financial goals with broader business objectives, creating a cohesive strategy that supports sustainable growth. Strategic financial planning sessions bring together key stakeholders, fostering collaboration and ensuring that everyone is on the same page. Cross-departmental financial alignment breaks down silos, promoting a unified approach to cost management that enhances efficiency and drives results.

Crafting a robust financial plan requires a strategic approach, beginning with setting clear financial objectives. These objectives serve as your guiding light, directing your efforts and resources toward achieving specific outcomes. Identifying cost-saving opportunities involves a thorough analysis of your current operations, pinpointing areas where efficiency can be improved. Once you've identified these opportunities, the next step is allocating resources efficiently. It's about prioritizing investments that offer the greatest return while minimizing waste. This process demands a keen eye for detail and a willingness to make tough decisions, but the payoff is a leaner, more agile business that's better equipped to compete in the marketplace.

The tools and technologies available today offer invaluable support in the financial planning process. Financial modeling software allows you to simulate various scenarios, providing insights into potential outcomes and helping you make informed decisions. Real-time data analytics tools offer a wealth of information at your fingertips, enabling you to monitor performance and adjust your strategy as needed. These technologies provide a level of precision and agility that was once unimaginable, allowing you to stay ahead of the curve and respond quickly to changing conditions. By leveraging these tools, you can enhance the accuracy and effectiveness of your financial planning, ensuring you're always one step ahead in the cost management game.

Interactive Element: Financial Planning Checklist

To help you get started, here's a simple checklist to guide you through the financial planning process. Use this as a roadmap to set financial objectives, identify cost-saving opportunities, and allocate resources efficiently. As you work through this checklist, consider how each step aligns with your strategic goals and enhances your overall business strategy. This practical tool is designed to help you implement the concepts discussed in this chapter, supporting your journey toward effective financial planning and cost management.

1.4 Building a Cost-Conscious Organizational Culture

Creating a cost-conscious culture within your organization isn't just a nice-to-have; it's a critical element for sustainable cost management. When everyone, from your entry-level employees to top executives, understands the value of every dollar spent, you build a foundation for long-term financial health. Consider a bustling office where every team member is keenly aware of their role in managing costs. They understand that turning off lights in unused rooms or opting for a video call instead of a business trip can save significant amounts over time. This mindset nurtures accountability, ensuring each employee feels responsible for the company's financial well-being. Implementing cost-awareness programs can serve as a reminder of this shared responsibility, fostering a collaborative approach to cost management.

To embed this mindset throughout your organization, regular cost review meetings become vital. They offer a platform to discuss financial performance openly, evaluate spending patterns, and brainstorm cost-saving ideas. These meetings can transform cost management from a top-down directive into a collective effort. Employee training workshops on cost management further reinforce this culture by equipping staff with the necessary skills and knowledge to identify cost-saving opportunities in their daily tasks. You might consider workshops that focus on practical skills, like efficient resource allocation or negotiating better terms with suppliers. This hands-on approach empowers employees to make informed decisions that align with the organization's financial goals.

Leadership plays a pivotal role in promoting a cost-conscious culture. Leaders must lead by example, demonstrating fiscal responsibility in their actions and decisions. When leaders champion cost-saving initiatives and communicate their importance, it sets a tone that resonates throughout the organization. Incentivizing cost-saving initiatives can further motivate employees to contribute actively. Consider implementing recognition programs that celebrate cost-saving achievements, whether that's by highlighting successful projects in company newsletters or offering bonuses for innovative ideas that significantly reduce expenses. Transparent communication of cost goals is also crucial. When employees understand the company's financial objectives and how their contributions matter, they are more likely to engage and invest in the process.

The benefits of cultivating a cost-conscious culture are far-reaching. Financial performance improves as cost-saving measures become ingrained in everyday operations, leading to reduced expenses and increased profitability. But it's not just about the numbers. Increased employee engagement is another key advantage. When employees feel involved in the financial success of the organization, they are more motivated, leading to higher productivity and job satisfaction. This engagement creates a positive feedback loop where employees continue to seek ways to save money and improve efficiency, perpetuating a culture of cost-consciousness. Ultimately, this culture becomes a powerful driver for innovation and competitive advantage, positioning your company for success in an ever-evolving business landscape.

1.5 Metrics that Matter: Key Performance Indicators for Cost Management

In the quest to master cost management, key performance indicators (KPIs) are indispensable. They act as the compass guiding your business decisions, ensuring you maintain the right course toward financial health. Among the myriad of KPIs, certain ones stand out for their ability to illuminate cost management: cost variance analysis, return on investment (ROI), and total cost of ownership (TCO). Each of these metrics provides a unique lens through which to evaluate cost efficiency and project cost-effectiveness. Picture a construction company juggling various projects. Here, cost variance analysis might reveal discrepancies between budgeted and actual expenses, signaling where adjustments are needed. ROI, on the other hand, offers a snapshot of the profitability of investments, helping prioritize funding. Meanwhile, TCO provides a comprehensive view of the total cost incurred over the lifecycle of an asset, crucial for long-term financial planning. Together, these KPIs form a trifecta that empowers businesses to manage costs with precision.

The significance of each of these KPIs lies in its capacity to measure different facets of cost management success. Cost variance analysis is invaluable in assessing cost efficiency. It highlights areas where costs deviate from expectations, enabling swift corrective action. ROI is the go-to metric for assessing the cost-effectiveness of projects. It quantifies the gains from investments relative to their costs, guiding strategic decisions on resource allocation. TCO, meanwhile, sheds light on the cumulative costs associated with acquiring, operating, and disposing of an asset. By understanding these expenses, businesses can make informed decisions about asset management and strategic planning. These KPIs not only provide insight into current performance but also inform future strategies, ensuring that cost management efforts align with broader business objectives.

Selecting the right KPIs is crucial for effective cost management. It's not a one-size-fits-all process; rather, it requires a thoughtful approach that considers the unique context of your business. Alignment with strategic objectives is paramount. For instance, if your goal is to enhance operational efficiency, KPIs should reflect this, perhaps focusing on cost variance and TCO. Relevance to industry benchmarks is another key consideration. Comparing your performance against industry standards provides valuable context and helps identify areas for improvement. Lastly, flexibility is essential. Business environments are dynamic, and KPIs must adapt to changing conditions to remain relevant and useful. By carefully selecting KPIs, you ensure that your cost management efforts are both targeted and effective.

The tools at your disposal for tracking and analyzing KPIs are more sophisticated than ever, offering invaluable support in managing costs. Business intelligence software is a powerful ally, enabling you to collect, analyze, and visualize data with ease. These tools provide real-time insights into your financial performance, allowing you to make informed decisions quickly. Performance dashboards further enhance your ability to monitor KPIs. They offer a consolidated view of key metrics, making it easy to track progress and identify trends. With these tools, you gain the ability to manage costs proactively, addressing issues before they impact your bottom line. By leveraging technology, you transform cost management from a reactive process into a strategic one, positioning your business for long-term success.

Textual Element: Reflection Section - Evaluating Your KPIs

Take a moment to reflect on the KPIs currently in use within your organization. Are they aligned with your strategic objectives? Do they offer the insights needed to manage costs effectively? If not, consider revisiting your selection criteria. This reflection section is an opportunity to evaluate and refine your approach, ensuring that your KPIs provide the clarity and direction needed to achieve your financial goals. By continually assessing your metrics, you keep your cost management strategy agile and responsive to the ever-evolving business landscape.

1.6 Strategic Cost Allocation Across Departments

Strategic cost allocation is the process of distributing costs across various departments in a way that optimizes the use of resources and reduces waste. Think of it as the financial equivalent of a well-choreographed dance, where each department knows its part and moves in harmony with others. By strategically allocating costs, businesses can improve resource efficiency, ensuring that every dollar is spent where it's most needed. This approach also enhances financial transparency, making it easier for decision-makers to understand where resources are being utilized and where adjustments might be necessary.

One effective method for cost allocation is activity-based costing (ABC). This technique allocates costs based on the activities that drive them, providing a more accurate picture of resource consumption. For example, in a manufacturing company, ABC might reveal that a significant portion of costs comes from machine setup and maintenance, prompting a review of these processes for potential savings. Zero-based budgeting is another powerful tool, where each department starts from zero and justifies every expense anew, ensuring no funds are allocated without a clear purpose. Departmental cost centers can also be employed, where each department is treated as a separate entity with its own budget, promoting accountability and encouraging efficient resource use.

Despite its benefits, strategic cost allocation isn't without challenges. Maintaining accuracy in cost distribution can be tricky, especially in complex organizations with interdependent departments. A common pitfall is the misallocation of shared costs, such as overheads, which can lead to disputes and inefficiencies. Addressing inter-departmental conflicts requires clear communication and a willingness to collaborate. Solutions might include establishing a cross-functional team tasked with overseeing cost allocation, ensuring that all departments are represented and have a voice in the process. Regular audits and reviews can also help maintain accuracy, providing an opportunity to adjust allocations as needed and resolve any discrepancies.

The impact of strategic cost allocation on financial decision-making is profound. By providing a clear picture of where resources are being used, it informs data-driven budgeting, allowing leaders to make informed decisions that align with strategic goals. Enhanced accountability in resource use means that departments are more likely to stay within budget and seek cost-saving opportunities. This, in turn, fosters a culture of financial responsibility, where every team member understands the importance of managing resources wisely. As a result, businesses can navigate challenges with agility, seizing opportunities for growth while minimizing unnecessary expenditures.

Strategic cost allocation is a powerful tool that can transform how businesses operate. By optimizing resource use and enhancing financial transparency, it lays the groundwork for more informed decision-making and a more efficient organization. As you consider implementing these strategies in your own business, think about how they can be tailored to meet your unique needs and goals. Whether you're a financial manager, a C-suite executive, or an entrepreneur, strategic cost allocation offers a path to greater efficiency and profitability. Embrace this approach, and you're likely to see significant improvements in how your organization manages its resources, paving the way for sustainable success.

NOTES:

Chapter 2: Cost-Saving Strategies Across Departments

Imagine you're at the helm of a ship navigating through unpredictable waters. The key to reaching your destination isn't just about having the wind at your back; it's about trimming the sails and steering efficiently. In business, this translates to streamlining your operations and cutting unnecessary costs. Procurement stands as one of the most significant areas where strategic adjustments can yield substantial savings. Think of it not merely as buying goods but as crafting a symphony where every note and pause must be carefully orchestrated.

2.1 Streamlining Procurement for Maximum Savings

Start by evaluating your current procurement processes. Picture a bustling marketplace where every vendor is eager for your attention. Now, imagine having a clear map of that market, highlighting the best stalls for quality and value. Conducting supplier audits helps you identify which vendors provide the best bang for your buck. It's like having a trusted local guide who knows where to find the freshest produce without breaking the bank. Procurement cycle time analysis is your stopwatch, helping you track how long it takes from placing an order to receiving goods. The shorter the cycle, the less cash tied up in transit, freeing resources for other ventures.

Negotiating better terms with suppliers can be a game-changer. Consider the impact of long-term agreements. Much like committing to a favorite gym, you might find that suppliers are willing to offer better rates for your loyalty. Volume discounts play a similar role. When you purchase in bulk, suppliers often shave off the price, rewarding you for reducing their sales efforts. It's akin to buying your coffee beans in bulk—each cup costs less, and your morning brew tastes just as good, if not better.

Implementing strategic sourcing practices is another powerful lever. Category management in sourcing allows you to group similar items and seek the best deals across the board, much like a savvy shopper using a list to avoid impulse buys. Online procurement platforms serve as your digital marketplace, offering a transparent view of options and prices. They streamline the process, making it more efficient and less prone to human error. It's like shopping online for a new appliance and being able to compare prices and reviews all in one place.

Leveraging technology in procurement is akin to having a smart assistant who knows your preferences and makes recommendations. E-procurement systems automate routine tasks, reducing errors and freeing up your team to focus on strategic decisions. Supplier relationship management software offers a comprehensive view of your supplier interactions, helping you track performance and identify areas for improvement. It's like having a digital Rolodex that not only stores contacts but also tracks every conversation and transaction, ensuring you always have the upper hand in negotiations.

Textual Element: Checklist - Enhancing Your Procurement Strategy

To get started, here's a quick checklist to ensure your procurement strategy is on track. Conduct regular supplier audits to maintain quality and cost-effectiveness. Analyze procurement cycle times to minimize delays and optimize cash flow. Negotiate long-term agreements and volume discounts to secure better pricing. Implement category management to streamline sourcing and reduce costs. Leverage online platforms to enhance transparency and efficiency. Utilize e-procurement and supplier relationship management tools to automate processes and improve supplier interactions. Reflect on each item and consider how these strategies can be tailored to fit your unique business needs.

Incorporating these strategies into your procurement processes can transform a routine task into a powerful driver of efficiency and savings. By focusing on these critical areas, you not only enhance your bottom line but also position your business for sustained growth and success.

2.2 Optimizing Manufacturing Processes for Cost Efficiency

In the manufacturing world, optimizing processes isn't just about cutting costs—it's about building a lean, mean production machine. Adopting lean manufacturing techniques can revolutionize how you operate. Lean principles, like minimizing waste and maximizing productivity, are at the heart of this transformation. A key element of lean is the just-in-time inventory system. Imagine running a factory where parts arrive precisely when needed, eliminating excess stock and reducing storage costs. It's like having groceries delivered exactly when you plan to cook, ensuring freshness and freeing up space. Alongside this, adopting Kaizen, or continuous improvement, means fostering an environment where everyone contributes to ongoing enhancements. This culture empowers employees to suggest small, incremental changes that collectively lead to significant improvements in efficiency and quality.

Automation plays a pivotal role in reducing manual labor costs and enhancing operational efficiency. Think of robotics in assembly lines as tireless workers who never need a coffee break, consistently delivering high-quality output at a fraction of the time it would take manually. Automated quality control systems further streamline production by quickly identifying defects, ensuring that only products meeting your standards leave the factory. This proactive approach reduces the cost of rework and returns, boosting your bottom line. Imagine a bakery where robots handle the repetitive task of kneading dough, freeing up skilled bakers to focus on crafting new recipes. By automating mundane tasks, you allow your workforce to focus on innovation and value-added activities, driving productivity to new heights.

Effective production scheduling is another cornerstone of cost-efficient manufacturing. It's crucial to ensure that every machine, every worker, and every minute counts. Capacity planning tools help you predict demand and adjust resources accordingly, preventing costly downtime or overproduction. Real-time production tracking offers a live dashboard of your operations, allowing you to spot bottlenecks and adjust on the fly. Picture this scenario: a factory where managers can see, in real-time, which machines are running below capacity or where a delay might affect the entire line. With this insight, they can make informed decisions to optimize resource use and maintain a seamless flow in production, ensuring that every cog in the machine operates in harmony.

Regular maintenance and equipment upgrades are vital to preventing unexpected breakdowns and costly repairs. Predictive maintenance technologies allow you to monitor equipment health in real-time, scheduling repairs before a minor issue becomes a major disruption. It's like taking your car for a check-up before a long road trip, ensuring it's in top shape to handle the journey. Investing in energy-efficient machinery is another smart move. Not only does it reduce energy consumption and lower utility bills, but it also aligns with sustainable practices that appeal to eco-conscious consumers. Consider a factory floor where machines hum with precision, optimized for peak performance and minimal energy use. By keeping your equipment updated and well-maintained, you ensure that your manufacturing processes remain efficient, reliable, and cost-effective.

Lean manufacturing, automation, strategic scheduling, and regular maintenance all contribute to a streamlined, cost-efficient production process. Each plays a vital role in reducing waste, improving quality, and boosting productivity. By integrating these strategies, you create a manufacturing environment where efficiency and innovation thrive. It's not just about cutting costs—it's about building a resilient, agile operation capable of adapting to changing market demands and seizing new opportunities. In the end, optimizing your manufacturing processes leads to a more competitive, profitable business that stands the test of time.

2.3 Reducing Overheads in Administrative Functions

Let's talk about the often-overlooked area of administrative overheads. In many organizations, these costs can quietly inflate the budget, much like a balloon slowly being filled. Start by conducting an overhead cost audit. This is your magnifying glass to spot non-essential expenses lurking in the shadows. Take office supplies, for instance. They might seem like small potatoes, but when you add up all those sticky notes, pens, and paper clips, it can amount to a hefty sum. Analyze your usage and consider setting up a central supply area to monitor and manage consumption more effectively. Then look at your utility bills.

Are there lights left on after hours, or is the office climate set to tropical in the winter? Simple adjustments here can lead to significant savings over time.

Now, consider remote work policies as a means to trim costs. The pandemic has taught us that many administrative tasks can be efficiently handled from home. Encouraging remote work can lead to a reduction in office space needs and associated costs. Offer home office setup allowances to ensure employees have everything they need to be productive at home. This small investment can pay dividends in reduced office expenditures. Virtual collaboration tools like Zoom or Microsoft Teams facilitate seamless communication, ensuring that being apart doesn't mean being disconnected. This shift not only saves on physical space but also opens the doors to a wider talent pool, no longer confined by geography.

Making the most of your office space is another way to cut down on overheads. If parts of your office are gathering dust, consider optimizing that space. Hot-desking arrangements, where employees use any available desk rather than having assigned seating, can reduce the amount of space needed. This approach is especially effective if you have a workforce that spends a significant amount of time out of the office or working remotely. Additionally, subleasing unused office space can turn a potential cost into a revenue stream. By maximizing every square foot, you ensure that your office is a hub of productivity and not a drain on resources.

Automation of administrative tasks is a fantastic way to improve efficiency and reduce costs. Think about the repetitive tasks that bog down your admin staff—scheduling meetings, managing documents, or processing invoices. Electronic document management systems can streamline these processes, reducing the need for physical storage and minimizing the risk of lost paperwork. Similarly, automated scheduling software can handle appointments and reminders, freeing up your team to focus on more strategic activities. With automation, you create a leaner, more agile administrative function that supports the broader goals of the organization.

By examining these areas, you not only reduce costs but also create a more dynamic and adaptable administrative environment. This approach empowers your team to focus on adding value rather than managing mundane tasks. It's about making smart choices that align with your strategic goals and support the financial health of your business. Embracing these strategies can transform your administrative operations, making them a cornerstone of efficiency and cost-effectiveness.

2.4 Enhancing Marketing Efficiency Without Sacrificing Impact

Marketing is often seen as the creative heart of a business, but it doesn't have to be a budget drain to be effective. By embracing data-driven marketing strategies, you can sharpen your focus and reduce wasted spend. Imagine you're setting out on a road trip. Instead of blindly guessing your route, you use a GPS to guide you with pinpoint accuracy. That's what customer segmentation analysis does for your marketing efforts. By understanding who your customers are and what they want, you target your campaigns more effectively. Predictive marketing analytics takes it a step further, using data to forecast future buying behaviors. It's like having a crystal ball that helps you anticipate customer needs and adapt your strategies accordingly.

Optimizing digital marketing channels can also deliver high returns without breaking the bank. Consider search engine optimization (SEO) as your secret weapon. By ensuring your website ranks high on search engines, you can drive organic traffic without paying for ads. It's the equivalent of having a prime storefront location without the hefty rent. Meanwhile, social media advertising optimization allows you to reach your audience where they spend most of their time. By crafting engaging ads and targeting them to the right demographics, you maximize engagement and conversion rates. It's like throwing a house party where only your closest friends are invited, ensuring a fun and fruitful gathering.

Content marketing is another cost-efficient way to engage with your audience. Think of it as storytelling with a purpose, where you share valuable insights that resonate with your customers. Blogging and thought leadership content establish your brand as an authority in your field, building trust and loyalty. Imagine you're at a dinner party, and the conversation turns to your area of expertise. You share your knowledge, impressing fellow guests and leaving a lasting impression. Video marketing on budget platforms, like YouTube or TikTok, provides a dynamic way to connect with your audience. These videos don't need to be Hollywood productions; authenticity often wins the day. It's about engaging your audience with relatable content that conveys your message effectively.

To ensure your marketing efforts hit the mark, implementing performance-based marketing metrics is crucial. These metrics act as your dashboard, providing real-time insights into your campaigns' effectiveness. Marketing ROI measurements help you understand the return on your investment for each campaign, much like checking your bank statement to see how your savings are growing. Conversion rate optimization techniques focus on turning website visitors into customers. By analyzing user behavior and making data-driven adjustments, you enhance the user experience and increase conversions. It's akin to refining a recipe—tweaking ingredients and techniques until you achieve the perfect balance of flavors.

By leveraging these strategies, you create a marketing machine that's both efficient and impactful. You engage your audience with precision, making every dollar count. In a world where marketing budgets are often under scrutiny, these approaches allow you to deliver results that speak for themselves, ensuring your brand stands out in a crowded marketplace.

2.5 IT Cost Optimization: Balancing Technology and Budget

In the fast-paced world where technology drives nearly every aspect of operations, keeping a firm grip on IT costs can be a formidable challenge. It's crucial to assess your current IT expenditures with a fine-tooth comb. Conducting software licensing audits is a great starting point. Often, organizations pay for licenses they no longer use or need, much like paying for multiple streaming services when you only watch shows on one. By identifying these unused licenses, you

18

can immediately free up funds for more strategic initiatives. Similarly, a cloud service usage analysis can reveal inefficiencies. Cloud services, while incredibly flexible, can rack up costs if not monitored closely. Think of it as leaving the lights on in every room of a house—unnecessary and costly. By optimizing cloud usage, you ensure you're only paying for what you actively use, avoiding surprise bills.

Adopting cloud computing solutions presents a golden opportunity to slash IT infrastructure costs. Cloud-based data storage eliminates the need for maintaining bulky physical servers, reducing both hardware expenses and the associated maintenance overhead. Imagine a cluttered basement full of unused equipment—going cloud-based is like clearing that space for better use. SaaS (Software as a Service) applications also offer a cost-effective alternative to traditional software purchases. Instead of hefty upfront investments, SaaS applications provide a subscription model that allows for easy scaling, ensuring you pay only for what you need, when you need it. This flexibility not only cuts costs but also enables businesses to stay agile and responsive to changing demands.

Cybersecurity remains a top priority, yet it doesn't have to drain the budget. Implementing multi-factor authentication provides an additional layer of security, akin to locking your front door and setting a security alarm, without the high price tag. Utilizing open-source security tools can be a game-changer, offering robust protection without the hefty fees of commercial software. These tools are often community-driven, meaning they benefit from constant updates and improvements at little to no cost. The key is to strike a balance between robust security measures and cost-efficiency, ensuring your business is protected without overspending.

Promoting IT resource efficiency is another vital component of cost optimization. Virtualization of servers allows multiple virtual servers to run on a single physical server, maximizing resource use and reducing energy consumption. It's like carpooling for your servers—more economical and environmentally friendly. Automated IT asset management, meanwhile, streamlines the tracking and maintenance of your IT assets, from laptops to software licenses. By automating this process, you reduce human error and ensure timely updates and

19

renewals, avoiding costly lapses. Imagine having a digital assistant that reminds you when it's time to renew your car insurance or change your oil—it's that level of proactive management that keeps costs in check.

Incorporating these strategies into your IT operations not only reduces expenses but also enhances overall efficiency. By keeping a close eye on expenditures and leveraging cloud solutions, you maintain a lean, agile IT environment. Prioritizing cybersecurity without overspending ensures your data remains protected, while promoting resource efficiency keeps your IT infrastructure running smoothly. These practices help you balance technology needs with budget constraints, supporting your business's growth and success in an increasingly digital world.

2.6 Cross-Departmental Collaboration for Unified Cost Control

In any thriving business, departments often resemble the various instruments of an orchestra. Each department plays its part, but without a conductor, the music can quickly become discordant. Effective inter-departmental communication acts as that conductor, ensuring harmony in the pursuit of shared cost-saving goals. Cross-functional team meetings are the rehearsals where departments come together, sharing insights and aligning strategies. Imagine a production team collaborating with marketing to streamline product launches, reducing costs while maximizing impact. Centralized communication platforms further facilitate this collaboration, providing a digital stage where all departments have a voice. These platforms ensure that everyone is in sync, reducing miscommunication and fostering a culture of transparency.

Setting unified cost-saving goals is akin to composing a symphony. Each department contributes its unique notes, but together they create a powerful melody of efficiency and savings. Collaborative goal-setting sessions bring together representatives from each department to outline these objectives. During these sessions, teams discuss potential cost-saving measures and decide on shared targets. By aligning these goals with the overall business strategy, you ensure that every department is working towards a common vision. Integrated performance metrics serve as the sheet music, providing clear benchmarks for success and allowing for real-time adjustments. These metrics not only track progress but also highlight areas where collaboration is most effective, encouraging departments to continuously refine their approaches.

To truly unlock the potential of cross-departmental collaboration, it's vital to implement cross-training programs. These programs encourage skill-sharing across departments, enhancing flexibility and resource allocation. Job rotation schemes offer employees the chance to experience different roles, broadening their understanding and fostering a more cohesive workforce. Picture an HR manager spending a week with the sales team to better understand their challenges, leading to more tailored recruitment strategies. Inter-departmental workshops provide a platform for employees to share best practices and innovative ideas. By breaking down the silos that often separate departments, these programs create a more adaptable and resilient organization, ready to tackle any challenge that comes its way.

Developing a culture of shared responsibility is the final note in the symphony of collaboration. When every employee feels accountable for cost control, the entire organization benefits. Incentive programs for team-based savings motivate employees to actively seek out cost-saving opportunities. Recognizing collaborative achievements, whether through awards or public acknowledgment, reinforces the importance of working together towards common goals. This culture of shared responsibility not only enhances cost control but also boosts employee morale, creating a positive feedback loop that drives continuous improvement. By fostering an environment where collaboration is celebrated and rewarded, you cultivate a workforce that's engaged, motivated, and aligned with the company's financial objectives.

As we conclude this chapter on cost-saving strategies across departments, it's clear that collaboration is the linchpin of successful cost control. By fostering communication, setting unified goals, implementing cross-training, and developing a culture of shared responsibility, you create a cohesive and efficient organization. This collaborative approach not only reduces costs but also strengthens the bonds between departments, paving the way for a more integrated and dynamic business. In the next chapter, we'll explore how advanced financial management techniques can further enhance your organization's profitability, building on the foundation of collaboration and cost control established here.

NOTES:

Chapter 3: Advanced Financial Management Techniques

Picture your business finances as a garden. Without regular care, weeds can overrun, and plants can wither. Effective budget management is like a gardener's hand, nurturing growth and removing waste. In this chapter, we'll explore advanced techniques to optimize your budget, ensuring your resources are wisely allocated and your business thrives. It's not just about cutting costs—it's about channeling funds to fuel innovation and sustain growth. Whether you're a financial manager, C-suite executive, operations manager, or entrepreneur, mastering these techniques will empower you to make informed decisions that enhance your company's financial health.

Zero-based budgeting (ZBB) offers a revolutionary approach to budget management, starting with a clean slate and re-evaluating every expense from scratch. Traditional budgeting often carries forward past expenditures, assuming their necessity without scrutiny. ZBB challenges this norm, demanding justification for each dollar spent. Imagine opening your fridge and deciding what groceries to buy without assuming you'll need the same items as last week. This approach encourages a fresh look at your expenses, identifying what's truly essential versus what's merely habitual. By prioritizing strategic priorities and key performance indicators, ZBB aligns your financial resources with your business's core objectives, ensuring that every expense delivers value. Implementing ZBB requires a collaborative effort, with finance teams, business leaders, and HR working together to embrace change and focus on value delivery rather than mere cost-cutting (SOURCE 1).

Flexible budgeting techniques offer another layer of adaptability, allowing you to respond to changing business conditions with agility. Unlike static budgets, which can become quickly outdated, flexible budgets adjust as your business environment evolves. Rolling budgets are a prime example, continuously updating to reflect current financial realities. It's like having a GPS that recalibrates your route based on real-time traffic, ensuring you stay on course. Scenario-based budgeting takes this flexibility further, allowing you to plan for multiple outcomes. By preparing for best-case, worst-case, and expected scenarios, you equip your business to navigate uncertainty with confidence, adapting your financial strategies as needed.

Performance-based budgeting (PBB) aligns budget allocations with performance outcomes, ensuring resources are directed toward the most impactful areas. By linking budgets to departmental KPIs, PBB creates a clear connection between spending and results. It's akin to rewarding your garden's most fruitful plants with more water and sunlight. This approach incentivizes departments to focus on cost-effective performance, driving efficiency and accountability. PBB transforms budgeting from a routine task into a strategic tool, empowering departments to take ownership of their financial goals and deliver measurable results. By fostering a culture of accountability, PBB encourages continuous improvement and innovation across your organization.

Variance analysis serves as a critical tool for monitoring budget adherence, providing insights into where your financial plan is hitting the mark and where it may be veering off course. Monthly budget variance reports offer a snapshot of your financial performance, highlighting discrepancies between budgeted and actual expenses. When variances occur, they signal a need for corrective actions. Perhaps your marketing spend exceeded projections due to an unplanned campaign, or your production costs rose with raw material prices. By analyzing these variances, you identify patterns and make informed adjustments, ensuring your budget remains a living document that reflects your business's evolving needs.

Textual Element: Case Study - Embracing Zero-Based Budgeting

Consider the example of a mid-sized tech company that implemented zero-based budgeting to revitalize its financial strategy. Initially skeptical, the leadership team was surprised by the hidden costs revealed through this process. By questioning every expense, they discovered substantial savings in software licenses and subscriptions that were no longer necessary. This freed up funds for strategic investments in product development and employee training. The company experienced a 15% improvement in its profit margins within a year, demonstrating the transformative power of zero-based budgeting. This case study illustrates the potential of reimagining your budgeting approach, aligning it with strategic priorities and unlocking new opportunities for growth (SOURCE 1).

By integrating these advanced budgeting techniques, you cultivate a financial ecosystem where resources are optimized, performance is enhanced, and your business is poised for success. Embrace this strategic approach to budgeting, and watch your financial garden flourish.

3.2 Cash Flow Management for Sustained Financial Health

Cash flow is the lifeblood of your business. Managing it effectively ensures that you can meet your obligations, invest in growth, and weather any financial storms. The foundation of effective cash flow management lies in accurate forecasting. By predicting the inflows and outflows of cash, you can prevent liquidity issues that could disrupt operations. Short-term cash flow projections focus on immediate needs, ensuring you have enough cash to cover day-to-day expenses. These forecasts provide a snapshot of your financial health, helping you stay on top of bills, payroll, and unexpected expenses. On the other hand, long-term projections look further ahead, giving you a view of how your financial landscape might evolve. This helps in planning for investments, expansion, or seasonal fluctuations. Sensitivity analysis adds depth to these forecasts by considering various scenarios and their impact on your cash flow, allowing you to prepare for different outcomes and make informed decisions.

To enhance cash flow efficiency and stability, several strategies can be implemented. Accelerating receivables collection is a practical approach. By reducing the time it takes to receive payments from customers, you improve your cash inflow. This might involve offering discounts for early payments or implementing stricter credit terms. It's like speeding up the process of turning your sales into available cash, ensuring that your business has the necessary liquidity. Meanwhile, extending payables without incurring penalties can also boost your cash flow. By negotiating longer payment terms with suppliers, you

26

hold onto your cash for a longer period, improving your cash position. This strategy must be balanced carefully to maintain healthy supplier relationships while optimizing your cash resources.

Implementing cash flow monitoring systems is crucial for ongoing financial oversight. Real-time cash flow dashboards provide an up-to-date view of your cash position, allowing you to track inflows and outflows efficiently. These dashboards act like a financial compass, guiding your decisions and alerting you to any deviations from expected cash flow patterns. Automated alerts for cash flow thresholds offer an additional layer of protection. These alerts notify you when your cash balance approaches critical levels, enabling proactive measures to address potential shortfalls. By keeping a finger on the pulse of your cash flow, you ensure that your business remains agile and responsive to financial changes, reducing the risk of liquidity crises.

Cash reserves play a vital role in maintaining financial stability. Establishing minimum reserve requirements ensures that you have a safety net to fall back on during challenging times. Think of cash reserves as the rainy-day fund for your business, providing a cushion against unexpected expenses or economic downturns. By setting aside a portion of your earnings as reserves, you build a financial buffer that supports business continuity. Moreover, the strategic use of excess cash reserves can enhance your financial position. Instead of allowing excess cash to sit idle, consider using it to pay down debt, invest in growth opportunities, or improve operations. This strategic allocation of reserves not only strengthens your financial foundation but also positions your business for long-term success.

Interactive Element: Cash Flow Scenario Exercise

Now, let's put these concepts into practice with a cash flow scenario exercise. Imagine your business is facing a sudden increase in demand, requiring additional inventory purchases. Using your cash flow forecasts, determine how this demand will impact your short-term and long-term cash flows. Consider strategies to accelerate receivables and extend payables to manage this demand effectively. Reflect on how your cash reserves could support this situation, ensuring that your

27

business remains financially sound. This exercise will help you apply the techniques discussed in this chapter, reinforcing your understanding of cash flow management.

3.3 Leveraging Financial Forecasting for Strategic Planning

Imagine standing at the helm of your business, peering into the future with a telescope that reveals the financial landscape ahead. That's what financial forecasting does—it transforms uncertainty into informed anticipation. By integrating forecasts into your strategic planning, you can align your financial projections with your broader business objectives. This alignment ensures that every decision, from launching a new product to scaling operations, is backed by a clear understanding of potential outcomes. Forecasts guide your investment decisions, helping you allocate resources where they promise the most significant returns. It's like mapping out a long road trip: knowing your destination and planning each stop along the way ensures you reach your goals efficiently and effectively.

When it comes to forecasting methods, there's no one-size-fits-all solution. Different environments demand different approaches. Time-series analysis involves examining historical data to identify trends and patterns, allowing you to make predictions based on past performance. It's like reading a book where past chapters give you hints about how the story will unfold. On the other hand, the Delphi method relies on expert opinions to forecast future events. By gathering insights from a panel of experts, you can make informed predictions even in complex or uncertain situations. This approach is akin to consulting a panel of seasoned travelers before setting out on a new adventure, drawing on their experiences to guide your decisions.

Scenario planning adds an extra layer of depth to forecasting, enabling you to prepare for various possible futures. By considering best-case and worst-case scenarios, you create a flexible strategy that accounts for uncertainty. It's like packing both sunscreen and an umbrella for a trip, ensuring you're ready for any weather. Contingency planning further enhances this approach by outlining specific actions to take in response to different scenarios. This proactive mindset reduces risks and maximizes opportunities, allowing you to respond swiftly to changes in the business environment. By integrating scenario planning with forecasting, you build resilience into your strategic planning process, ensuring your business is prepared for whatever comes its way.

Technology plays a crucial role in enhancing the accuracy and efficiency of financial forecasting. Predictive analytics platforms use advanced algorithms to analyze data and generate insights, providing you with a detailed view of potential outcomes. These platforms act like a high-tech crystal ball, offering glimpses into the future based on data-driven analysis. Cloud-based forecasting solutions further streamline the process by providing access to real-time data and collaborative tools. With these solutions, your team can work together seamlessly, sharing insights and updating forecasts as new information becomes available. This collaborative approach ensures your forecasts remain relevant and accurate, empowering you to make informed decisions with confidence. By leveraging these technological tools, you transform forecasting from a manual, time-consuming task into a dynamic, strategic asset that drives business success.

Visual Element: Forecasting Techniques Infographic

To help you visualize the concepts discussed in this section, here's an infographic that outlines different forecasting techniques and their applications. This visual guide provides a quick reference to the various methods available, helping you choose the approach that best suits your business needs. Use this infographic as a tool to explore different forecasting options and consider how they can be integrated into your strategic planning process. By understanding the strengths and limitations of each technique, you can make informed decisions that enhance your forecasting efforts and support your business goals.

Financial forecasting is more than just predicting numbers on a spreadsheet; it's about creating a roadmap for your business's future. By linking forecasts to strategic objectives, exploring various forecasting methods, integrating scenario planning, and leveraging technology, you develop a comprehensive strategy that supports

29

sustainable growth and profitability. With these tools at your disposal, you're better equipped to navigate the complexities of the business world, ensuring your organization remains agile, informed, and ready for whatever challenges and opportunities lie ahead.

3.4 Risk Management in Cost-Reduction Strategies

Tackling cost reduction can feel a bit like walking a tightrope. On one side, you've got the allure of immediate savings, and on the other, the potential pitfalls of unintended consequences. In this balancing act, understanding the financial risks associated with aggressive cost-cutting measures is crucial. Take quality compromise risks, for example. Slashing costs might save money in the short term, but if it leads to inferior products or services, you could lose customers and damage your brand. Then there's the impact on employee morale. When cost-cutting translates to layoffs or reduced benefits, it can create a culture of fear and dissatisfaction, leading to decreased productivity and increased turnover. A happy team is a productive team, and maintaining morale is vital even when trimming the budget.

To minimize these risks, a diversified approach to cost reduction is essential. Instead of slashing expenses across the board, focus on areas where efficiency can be improved without sacrificing quality. Think of it as pruning a tree—carefully cutting back branches to promote healthy growth rather than hacking away indiscriminately. Diversifying cost-reduction initiatives allows you to spread the impact and avoid concentrating risks in one area. Meanwhile, engaging employees in the process can help maintain morale and foster a sense of shared responsibility. Encourage them to contribute ideas and recognize their efforts in achieving cost-saving goals. This inclusive approach not only reduces resistance to change but also taps into the collective wisdom of your team, uncovering innovative solutions that might otherwise go unnoticed.

Incorporating risk assessment into your financial planning is another critical step in managing these challenges. By evaluating the potential risks associated with cost-cutting decisions, you can make more informed choices that balance savings with long-term sustainability. Risk-adjusted return on investment (ROI) is a valuable tool in this process, allowing you to weigh the potential benefits of a cost-saving measure against its associated risks. This approach ensures that you're not just looking at the numbers but also considering the broader impact on your business. Financial risk scoring models offer another layer of insight, providing a structured framework for evaluating risks and prioritizing actions. By integrating these tools into your decision-making, you create a more resilient financial strategy that's prepared for both opportunities and challenges.

A range of risk management tools and frameworks can aid in identifying and managing financial risks effectively. SWOT analysis, which stands for strengths, weaknesses, opportunities, and threats, is a simple yet powerful tool for evaluating the potential risks and benefits of a cost-reduction strategy. By assessing these factors, you gain a comprehensive view of the landscape, helping you make informed decisions. Monte Carlo simulations offer a more advanced approach, using statistical modeling to predict the range of possible outcomes for a given decision. This method provides a detailed picture of potential risks and rewards, allowing you to plan for different scenarios and adjust your strategy accordingly. By leveraging these tools, you enhance your ability to manage risks proactively, ensuring that your cost-reduction efforts support your long-term business goals.

3.5 Financial Tools and Software for Enhanced Decision-Making

Navigating the complex world of financial data can often feel like trying to piece together a jigsaw puzzle without the right pieces. That's where financial tools and software come into play, acting as the missing pieces that complete the picture. Business intelligence solutions are one of the most powerful tools at your disposal. These systems collect and analyze data from various sources, providing insights that drive smarter decision-making. They allow you to see patterns and trends that might otherwise be hidden in mountains of data. Complementing these are data visualization tools, which transform raw numbers into digestible charts and graphs. Imagine sifting through endless spreadsheets trying to find a trend versus seeing it clearly mapped out in a colorful graph—visualization tools make complex data accessible and understandable, helping you make informed decisions quickly.

When it comes to budgeting and forecasting, the right software can simplify what might otherwise be a daunting process. Integrated financial management systems bring together all your financial data into a single platform. This integration ensures consistency and accuracy across your financial statements, budgets, and forecasts. It's like having a central hub where all your financial information lives, making it easy to access and analyze. Cloud-based budgeting platforms offer further flexibility, allowing you to update and access your financial plans from anywhere. This cloud connectivity means you're not tied to a single office or device, enhancing collaboration across teams and ensuring everyone is on the same page. By streamlining the budgeting and forecasting process, these tools free up time for more strategic activities, allowing you to focus on what truly matters—growing your business.

Monitoring financial performance in real-time is crucial for staying ahead of the game. Financial performance tracking software provides you with the tools you need to keep a finger on the pulse of your business. Performance dashboards offer a comprehensive view of your key financial metrics, allowing you to track progress against your goals with ease. These dashboards act like a financial cockpit, giving you the controls to navigate your business with precision. Key metric tracking applications go a step further, enabling you to set alerts and notifications for critical thresholds. This functionality ensures that you're always aware of any significant changes in your financial performance, allowing you to take swift action when needed. With real-time insights, you're better equipped to make proactive decisions, ensuring your business remains agile and responsive to changing conditions.

Scenario analysis and planning are indispensable for managing uncertainty and preparing for various potential futures. Specialized software aids in conducting scenario analysis, allowing you to model different business outcomes based on various assumptions. This process is akin to rehearsing for multiple plays, ensuring you're ready no matter which script unfolds. Decision support systems further enhance this capability by providing data-driven recommendations for each scenario. These systems act like a trusted advisor, offering insights based on comprehensive analysis and helping you choose the best course of action. By exploring different scenarios and planning accordingly, you build resilience into your business strategy, ensuring you're prepared for any challenges or opportunities that come your way.

3.6 Aligning Financial Goals with Business Objectives

Aligning financial management with business goals is like ensuring that every note in a symphony contributes to the overall harmony of the piece. It's crucial for achieving success because it ensures that all parts of the business are working towards the same vision. Imagine if your marketing team is set on aggressive growth while your finance team is focused solely on cost-cutting. The result can be a discordant effort that doesn't propel the company forward effectively. Consistency between financial and strategic plans ensures that resources are allocated in a way that supports the company's overarching goals. This synergy creates a seamless flow where financial targets are not just numbers on a spreadsheet but are directly tied to the business's vision and mission. This alignment empowers your organization to move with purpose and clarity, avoiding the pitfalls of miscommunication and misaligned priorities.

To achieve this harmony, integrated financial planning frameworks are key. They provide a structured approach to ensuring that financial strategies are aligned with business objectives. Consider the balanced scorecard approach, which translates a company's strategic objectives into a set of performance measures across different perspectives—financial, customer, internal processes, and learning and growth. This multi-dimensional view ensures that financial goals are not isolated but are part of a broader strategy that encompasses all aspects of the business. Similarly, Integrated Business Planning (IBP) models take it a step further by integrating financial planning with operational planning. This holistic approach ensures that everyone in the organization understands how their role contributes to the company's financial success, fostering a culture of accountability and collaboration.

33

Fostering collaboration between finance and other departments is essential in aligning goals. It's not enough for each team to understand their role; they must also see how they fit into the bigger picture. Joint financial strategy meetings offer a platform for departments to share their plans and align their strategies with the company's goals. These meetings encourage open communication, breaking down silos and promoting a unified approach to achieving business objectives. Collaborative goal-setting workshops further enhance this process by bringing together diverse perspectives to identify common goals and strategies. These workshops foster a sense of shared responsibility, where each department feels invested in the company's success. This collaborative spirit enhances innovation and problem-solving, as teams work together to find solutions that benefit the entire organization.

Measuring the success of alignment efforts is crucial to ensure that your strategies are effective. Alignment KPIs and metrics provide a tangible way to evaluate how well financial goals are aligned with business objectives. These metrics serve as a compass, guiding your efforts and highlighting areas for improvement. Feedback loops for continuous alignment improvement offer an opportunity to refine strategies based on real-world results. By regularly reviewing progress and adjusting plans, you can ensure that your organization remains agile and responsive to changing conditions. This iterative process fosters a culture of continuous improvement, where teams are encouraged to learn from their experiences and strive for excellence.

As we wrap up this chapter on advanced financial management techniques, it's clear that aligning financial goals with business objectives is a cornerstone of strategic success. By fostering collaboration, utilizing integrated planning frameworks, and continuously measuring progress, you create a cohesive organization that thrives on synergy. In the next chapter, we'll explore how these principles can be applied to optimize supply chain and operations, further enhancing your company's efficiency and profitability.

NOTES:

Chapter 4: Supply Chain and Operations Efficiency

In the dynamic landscape of modern business, efficiency in supply chain and operations is more than just a competitive edge—it's a necessity. As companies strive to deliver faster, better, and cheaper, the principles of lean manufacturing stand out as a beacon of operational excellence. Imagine a bustling factory floor where every movement is purposeful, every resource is optimized, and waste is a relic of the past. Lean manufacturing transforms this vision into reality, driving waste reduction and enhancing production efficiency. For anyone involved in the intricate dance of supply chain management, from financial managers to C-suite executives, lean principles offer a roadmap to achieving streamlined operations and bolstered profitability.

At the heart of lean manufacturing are several core concepts that guide the quest for efficiency. One of the most foundational is the Five S's: Sort, Set in order, Shine, Standardize, and Sustain. These principles create a systematic approach to workplace organization, ensuring that everything from tools to workflows is optimized for maximum productivity. Sort involves eliminating unnecessary items from the workspace, akin to decluttering your garage to make space for what truly matters. Set in order focuses on arranging tools and materials in a logical manner, much like organizing your kitchen so that everything you need is within easy reach. Shine keeps the workspace clean and orderly, preventing clutter from creeping back in. Standardize establishes consistent practices, ensuring that everyone follows the same procedures. Finally, Sustain ensures that these practices become ingrained habits, maintaining the gains achieved through the other four steps.

Value stream mapping is another powerful tool in the lean arsenal. It provides a visual representation of the entire production process, highlighting areas of waste and inefficiency. Picture a map that lays out your entire journey, showing not only the path but also the obstacles along the way. By identifying bottlenecks and redundancies, value stream mapping enables you to streamline operations and reduce lead times. It's like finding shortcuts on your daily commute, saving time and reducing frustration. This tool is especially valuable for financial managers and operations professionals seeking to optimize resource allocation and enhance productivity.

Lean manufacturing aims to eliminate several specific types of waste, each of which can erode efficiency and profitability. Overproduction is one such waste, where producing more than is needed ties up capital and resources. It's like baking dozens of cookies when only a handful are needed, leaving the rest to go stale. Defects and rework are another form of waste, causing delays and additional costs as flawed products are corrected. Excess inventory represents yet more waste, with unsold products occupying valuable space and capital. By targeting these areas, lean manufacturing helps businesses streamline operations, reduce costs, and improve quality.

Implementing lean tools and techniques is essential for realizing these benefits. Kanban systems, for example, provide a visual framework for managing workflow and inventory, ensuring that production is closely aligned with demand. Imagine a board with cards representing tasks, each moving through stages from start to finish. This system not only enhances visibility but also facilitates communication and collaboration across teams. Just-in-time (JIT) production is another critical technique, synchronizing production with customer demand to minimize inventory and reduce waste. It's like having groceries delivered just as you're running out, reducing the need for storage and ensuring freshness. These tools empower businesses to respond swiftly to changing conditions, maintaining efficiency and flexibility.

Measuring the impact of lean initiatives is crucial for continuous improvement. Process cycle efficiency (PCE) is a key metric, evaluating the ratio of value-added time to total cycle time. A higher PCE indicates a more efficient process, where the majority of time is spent on value-creating activities. Reducing lead times is another important measure, reflecting the speed at which products move through the production process. By monitoring these metrics, businesses can assess the effectiveness of their lean initiatives, identifying areas for further improvement and celebrating successes along the way.

Textual Element: Case Study - Lean Transformation in Action

Consider a mid-sized electronics manufacturer that embraced lean principles to transform its operations. Initially plagued by excessive inventory and frequent production delays, the company implemented value stream mapping to identify bottlenecks. By reconfiguring production lines and adopting JIT practices, they reduced lead times by 40% and cut inventory by half. Kanban systems facilitated communication, ensuring that materials were available precisely when needed. As a result, the company not only improved efficiency but also enhanced customer satisfaction through faster delivery times. This case study illustrates the transformative power of lean manufacturing, offering a blueprint for success in any industry.

4.2 Sourcing and Procurement: Cost-Effective Strategies

Let's talk about strategic sourcing—a pivotal element in achieving both cost savings and efficiency. It's not just about finding the cheapest supplier; it's about building strong, mutually beneficial relationships. Supplier relationship management (SRM) is key here. Think of it like nurturing a friendship where trust and communication are paramount. When you foster good relationships with suppliers, you gain more than just favorable terms; you gain allies who can help navigate challenges and ensure a steady supply chain. This approach empowers you to negotiate better deals, access exclusive discounts, and even collaborate on product innovations.

Total cost of ownership (TCO) analysis is another critical component of strategic sourcing. Here, you're not just looking at the initial purchase price but considering the entire lifecycle cost of a product or service. Picture buying a car; the sticker price is just one part of the equation. Maintenance, fuel, insurance, and resale value all factor into the total cost. Similarly, in procurement, TCO analysis helps you understand the long-term financial impact of your sourcing decisions, guiding you toward choices that align with your budget and strategic goals.

When selecting suppliers, establishing criteria that prioritize cost-effectiveness and reliability is crucial. Quality assessment criteria should be at the forefront. You're looking for suppliers who consistently deliver high-quality products that meet your standards. This involves scrutinizing their production processes, quality control measures, and even their reputation in the industry. Supplier risk analysis also plays a role here. Assessing potential risks—such as financial stability, political instability in the supplier's region, or even ethical considerations—helps you make informed decisions that safeguard your supply chain.

Negotiating procurement contracts that maximize savings and value requires a strategic approach. Fixed versus variable pricing models offer different benefits depending on your needs. Fixed pricing provides predictability, which is ideal for budgeting, while variable pricing can offer flexibility and potential savings if market conditions change. Performance-based contracts are another tool in your arsenal. By tying payment to specific performance metrics, you incentivize suppliers to meet or exceed expectations, ensuring you get the best value for your investment.

Incorporating sustainability into procurement practices isn't just good for the planet; it's good for business. Green sourcing initiatives encourage selecting suppliers committed to environmentally friendly practices, reducing your carbon footprint and appealing to eco-conscious consumers. Lifecycle cost analysis further supports sustainable procurement by evaluating the environmental impact of a product from cradle to grave. It's like choosing to invest in energy-efficient appliances that save money and reduce environmental impact over time. Integrating these practices into your procurement strategy not only enhances your brand's reputation but also contributes to long-term cost savings and operational efficiency.

By focusing on strategic sourcing, supplier relationship management, and sustainable practices, you position your business to thrive in an increasingly competitive and environmentally conscious market. This approach ensures that every procurement decision is aligned with your broader strategic goals, driving both profitability and sustainability.

4.3 Logistics Optimization: Streamlining Distribution Channels

38

Boosting the efficiency of your logistics operations starts with a meticulous analysis of your current processes. Imagine taking a magnifying glass to your supply chain, identifying bottlenecks that cause delays and inflate costs. These bottlenecks might be as obvious as a congested loading dock or as subtle as a time-consuming paperwork procedure. Spotting these roadblocks is the first step in smoothing out the flow of goods from your suppliers to your customers. Route optimization studies can be a game-changer here, using data to find the shortest, quickest, or most cost-effective paths for your shipments. Picture a delivery truck weaving through a city, guided by real-time traffic updates to avoid jams and cut down on fuel costs. This kind of optimization not only saves money but also improves customer satisfaction by ensuring timely deliveries.

A Transportation Management System (TMS) can revolutionize how you handle logistics by offering real-time shipment tracking and comprehensive analytics on carrier performance. With a TMS, you gain visibility into every step of your product's journey, from warehouse to doorstep. Imagine being able to track a package in real-time, knowing exactly where it is and when it will arrive. This transparency reduces the guesswork and allows for proactive problem-solving. Carrier performance analytics take this a step further, providing insights into which carriers consistently meet delivery targets and which fall short. By harnessing this data, you can negotiate better rates, hold carriers accountable, and ultimately reduce transportation costs.

Warehouse operations are another area ripe for optimization. Cross-docking practices can significantly streamline operations, reducing storage time and costs by transferring goods directly from incoming to outgoing shipments. It's like a relay race where the baton is passed seamlessly from one runner to the next, minimizing downtime. Automated storage and retrieval systems (AS/RS) can also enhance efficiency, using robotics and computer systems to store and retrieve items quickly and accurately. These systems reduce the need for manual labor and minimize errors, leading to faster turnaround times and lower operational costs. Imagine a warehouse where products are swiftly and precisely moved by a network of conveyor belts and robotic arms, ensuring that orders are fulfilled with speed and accuracy.

Third-party logistics (3PL) providers can play a crucial role in optimizing your distribution channels. These partners offer specialized expertise and resources that can enhance your logistics operations, allowing you to focus on your core business activities. Conducting a cost-benefit analysis of 3PL partnerships helps determine the value they bring compared to handling logistics in-house. Consider factors such as cost savings, flexibility, and scalability when evaluating these relationships. Strategic partnership development with 3PL providers can lead to improved service levels, expanded reach, and reduced costs. Think of it as outsourcing your logistics to a trusted partner who can navigate the complexities of supply chain management, ensuring your products reach their destination efficiently and reliably. By leveraging the strengths of 3PL partners, you can streamline your logistics operations, reduce overheads, and deliver better service to your customers.

4.4 Inventory Management Techniques for Cost Savings

Managing inventory effectively is like balancing a tightrope. Too much stock ties up capital, while too little can lead to missed sales opportunities. Inventory management best practices aim to strike that perfect balance. One such method is ABC analysis, which categorizes inventory based on its importance to your business. Imagine sorting your wardrobe by how often you wear each item. Similarly, with ABC analysis, 'A' items are high-value products that require tight control, while 'C' items are lower-value, needing less oversight. This approach helps prioritize resources and focus on what truly matters. Economic order quantity (EOQ) models provide another essential tool, determining the optimal order size that minimizes both ordering and holding costs. It's like finding the perfect grocery list that keeps your fridge stocked without waste.

Accurate demand forecasting plays a pivotal role in inventory management, ensuring you have the right products available when needed. Sales trend analysis examines historical data to identify patterns, helping anticipate future demand. It's like tracking weather forecasts to plan your wardrobe for the coming week. Seasonal demand adjustments further refine these predictions, accounting for fluctuations due to holidays or seasonal changes. By understanding these trends, you can adjust inventory levels proactively, reducing the risk of stockouts or excess stock. This foresight not only optimizes inventory but also enhances customer satisfaction by ensuring products are available when desired.

Technology offers powerful tools to streamline inventory management processes. Inventory management software, equipped with optimization algorithms, analyzes data to suggest ideal stock levels and reorder points. These algorithms act like a financial advisor, offering insights based on complex calculations. Cloud-based inventory systems provide additional benefits, allowing you to access real-time inventory data from anywhere. Picture having instant access to your warehouse from your smartphone, enabling you to make informed decisions on the go. This connectivity enhances collaboration across teams and ensures that everyone has access to the latest information, reducing errors and improving efficiency.

Just-in-time (JIT) inventory systems take efficiency to the next level by aligning inventory levels with actual demand. By integrating suppliers into JIT processes, you create a responsive supply chain that adjusts dynamically to changes in demand. It's like having a personal shopper who delivers items only when you need them, minimizing storage costs and reducing waste. A responsive supply chain design further supports this approach, ensuring that all elements—from suppliers to distribution—work in harmony. This flexibility not only reduces inventory holding costs but also enhances the overall agility of your operations, allowing you to respond swiftly to market changes and customer demands.

By embracing these inventory management techniques, you can transform your approach to stock control. From categorizing inventory with ABC analysis to leveraging technology for real-time insights, these strategies enable you to optimize inventory levels, reduce costs, and enhance efficiency. Whether you're a financial manager overseeing budgets or an entrepreneur scaling a business, these techniques offer valuable tools to support your financial goals and drive operational success.

4.5 The Role of Technology in Supply Chain Efficiency

In a world where speed and precision dictate success, digital transformation has become a game-changer for supply chains. Technologies like the Internet of Things (IoT) and blockchain are revolutionizing how we manage supply chains, adding layers of efficiency and transparency. Imagine IoT as a vast network of interconnected devices, each offering real-time data insights. With IoT, you can monitor everything from the temperature of perishable goods to the precise location of shipments. This constant flow of information allows for swift decision-making, reducing delays and minimizing waste. Blockchain, on the other hand, offers unparalleled transparency and traceability. Picture it as a digital ledger, recording every transaction and movement in a supply chain. This transparency builds trust among stakeholders and reduces the risk of fraud, ensuring that every component of your supply chain is accounted for and reliable.

Supply chain management software (SCMS) further enhances coordination and efficiency by integrating data across the entire supply chain. With SCMS, you can access a centralized platform where data from suppliers, manufacturers, and distributors converge. This integration breaks down silos, offering a holistic view of operations. Automated order processing within SCMS streamlines the flow of goods, reducing manual errors and speeding up transactions. Imagine a system where orders are processed with just a few clicks, freeing up valuable time for strategic planning. These platforms not only improve operational efficiency but also provide the agility needed to respond swiftly to market changes.

Predictive analytics takes supply chain decision-making to the next level by offering insights based on historical data and trends. Demand forecasting models, powered by predictive analytics, help you anticipate customer needs with remarkable accuracy. It's like having a crystal ball that reveals future demand patterns, allowing you to adjust inventory and production accordingly. This foresight minimizes stockouts and overproduction, optimizing resource allocation. Risk assessment analytics further bolster decision-making by identifying potential disruptions before they occur. By analyzing variables such as weather patterns or geopolitical shifts, you can proactively mitigate risks, ensuring your supply chain remains resilient.

Artificial intelligence (AI) is a powerful ally in optimizing supply chain processes. Through machine learning, AI can enhance demand planning by analyzing vast datasets and identifying patterns that humans might overlook. This capability allows for more accurate forecasting and better alignment of supply with demand. AI-driven logistics optimization goes a step further, using algorithms to develop efficient routes and schedules. Imagine AI as a master strategist, continuously refining logistics operations to minimize costs and maximize speed. By leveraging AI, you can not only improve operational efficiency but also gain a competitive edge in a fast-paced business environment.

4.6 Building Resilient and Cost-Effective Supply Chains

In today's fast-paced business environment, supply chain resilience isn't just a buzzword; it's a vital strategy for ensuring stability and profitability. Think of resilience as your supply chain's ability to bend but not break under pressure. This flexibility means having adaptable networks that can quickly respond to unexpected disruptions. For example, if a primary supplier suddenly can't deliver due to unforeseen circumstances, a resilient supply chain seamlessly shifts to alternatives without missing a beat. Redundancy planning plays a crucial role here, acting like a safety net that catches the business when the unexpected happens. This involves having backup suppliers, alternative transport routes, and contingency plans that allow operations to continue smoothly.

But what are the risks that threaten supply chain operations? One significant vulnerability is supplier dependency. Relying too heavily on a single supplier can leave you in a pinch if they face issues like financial troubles or natural disasters. Imagine building a house of cards where one wrong move causes a collapse. Similarly, geopolitical factors can ripple through global supply chains, causing disruptions that impact everything from manufacturing to delivery. Tariffs, trade wars, or political unrest can create bottlenecks that affect the flow of goods and services, requiring rapid adaptation to maintain operations. Recognizing these risks is the first step towards building a more resilient supply chain that can withstand and adapt to such challenges.

To strengthen supply chain resilience, strategic diversification of your supplier base is key. By engaging multiple suppliers, you reduce the risk associated with any single point of failure. It's like investing in a diverse portfolio rather than putting all your eggs in one basket. Risk management frameworks provide a structured approach to identifying and mitigating potential disruptions. These frameworks guide you in assessing risks, developing contingency plans, and regularly reviewing strategies to ensure they remain effective. By proactively managing risks, you position your supply chain to navigate uncertainties with confidence, minimizing disruptions and maintaining a steady flow of goods and services.

Collaboration across the supply chain is another pillar of resilience. Collaborative planning, forecasting, and replenishment (CPFR) involves sharing information with key partners to align production and inventory with actual demand. It's like a well-rehearsed orchestra where every musician knows their part, creating harmony and efficiency. Strategic alliances with key partners further bolster resilience by fostering mutual support and shared goals. These alliances can lead to joint problem-solving, shared resources, and innovative solutions that enhance the overall strength of the supply chain. By working together, businesses can overcome challenges that would be insurmountable alone, creating a resilient and adaptable network that benefits all parties involved.

When evaluating the cost-benefit of resilience investments, it's important to consider both immediate and long-term impacts. A cost-benefit analysis of redundancy measures helps you weigh the upfront costs against the potential savings from avoiding disruptions. While redundancy may involve additional expenses, the long-term benefits of operational stability and continuity often outweigh the initial investment. By ensuring that critical components of your supply chain are shielded from disruptions, you protect your business from costly

44

downtimes and maintain customer satisfaction. Investing in resilience is not just about safeguarding against risks; it's about creating a competitive advantage that allows your business to thrive in an unpredictable world.

NOTES:

Chapter 5: Technology and Innovation in Cost Management

Imagine your business running like a finely tuned orchestra, where each instrument plays its part perfectly, creating a symphony of efficiency and profitability. This is the promise of automation in today's business landscape. Automation not only reduces manual effort but also enhances precision and speed, allowing you to focus on what truly matters—innovation and growth. In this chapter, we'll explore how automation can transform routine processes, offering significant cost savings and efficiency gains.

Automation is a game-changer for businesses. By automating routine tasks, you can significantly reduce manual errors, which are often costly and time-consuming to fix. Imagine a world where data entry errors are a thing of the past. Automation ensures that tasks are performed consistently and accurately, reducing the need for rework and saving valuable time. Additionally, automation increases processing speed, allowing your business to operate at a pace that keeps up with or even exceeds market demands. This boost in efficiency can be the difference between meeting a deadline and missing an opportunity.

To harness the benefits of automation, it's crucial to identify which business processes are ripe for automation. Inventory management is a prime candidate. By automating inventory tracking, you can maintain optimal stock levels, reducing carrying costs and minimizing the risk of stockouts or overstocking. Automated customer service interactions, such as chatbots, can handle routine inquiries, freeing up human agents to focus on more complex issues. This not only improves response times but also enhances customer satisfaction. Payroll and HR processes, often bogged down by paperwork, can be streamlined through automation, ensuring timely and accurate salary disbursements and compliance with regulations.

Implementing automation technologies requires careful planning and execution. Start by selecting the appropriate automation software that aligns with your business needs and objectives. Consider factors such

47

as scalability, integration capabilities, and user-friendliness. Once the software is chosen, invest in workforce training to ensure your team is equipped to use the new tools effectively. This step is crucial; the best technology is only as good as the people using it. Providing thorough training and support helps ease the transition and maximizes the potential benefits of automation. Clear communication about the changes and their expected impact also helps in gaining buy-in from employees.

Measuring the impact of automation is essential to understand its effectiveness and identify areas for further improvement. Time savings analysis can provide insights into how much time is freed up for more value-added activities. By comparing the time taken to complete tasks before and after automation, you can quantify the efficiency gains. Cost reduction metrics are equally important. Tracking the reduction in labor costs, error-related expenses, and other operational costs can paint a clear picture of the financial benefits achieved through automation. These metrics serve as a feedback loop, guiding future automation efforts and ensuring that your business continues to operate at peak efficiency.

Interactive Element: Automation Suitability Checklist

To help you identify processes in your organization that are suitable for automation, here's a checklist to guide your evaluation. Consider factors such as the volume and complexity of tasks, potential for error reduction, and impact on customer experience. Reflect on each item and assess how automation can enhance these processes within your business. This checklist is designed to support your decision-making process as you explore the transformative potential of automation.

Using Data Analytics to Identify Cost-Saving Opportunities

In today's data-driven world, the role of data analytics in cost management can't be overstated. Imagine your business as a sprawling city, with data acting as the network of roads connecting various districts. By tapping into this network, data analytics uncovers hidden cost-saving opportunities that might otherwise remain buried beneath layers of routine operations. It identifies cost patterns, revealing insights into spending habits that might have gone unnoticed. For example, analytics might show that a particular supplier consistently delivers products late, causing costly delays. With this information, you can renegotiate terms or explore alternative vendors. Predictive analytics goes a step further, providing forecasts that help you anticipate future costs and prepare accordingly, much like a weather app predicting a storm, so you know when to carry an umbrella.

Big data is like a treasure trove, offering deeper insights into your business's cost structures. When you integrate multiple data sources, you gain a holistic view of your operations, making it easier to pinpoint inefficiencies. Imagine combining sales data with inventory levels and customer feedback. This integration can highlight which products are flying off the shelves and which are gathering dust, allowing you to adjust purchasing and marketing strategies accordingly. Advanced data visualization tools play a critical role here, transforming complex datasets into intuitive charts and graphs. These visualizations make it easy to spot trends and outliers, empowering you to make informed decisions with confidence. It's like having a detailed map of that city, showing you exactly where the traffic jams are and how to avoid them.

Data-driven decision-making is about letting insights guide your strategies. Real-time data dashboards act as your command center, providing up-to-the-minute information at a glance. With these dashboards, you can monitor key performance indicators, track spending, and adjust strategies as needed. It's akin to having a GPS that updates you on your route, helping you steer clear of potential pitfalls. Data-driven strategy sessions bring your team together to collaborate on decisions based on solid evidence. During these sessions, you can brainstorm new initiatives, test hypotheses, and refine your approach, ensuring that every decision is backed by data rather than guesswork. By embedding data into your decision-making processes, you create a culture that values evidence over intuition, leading to more effective and efficient operations.

The power of data analytics is best illustrated through real-world examples. Consider a retail chain that leveraged analytics to optimize

49

its cost structure. By analyzing customer purchase patterns and inventory turnover, they identified slow-moving products and adjusted their buying strategy, reducing excess stock and freeing up capital. This data-driven approach led to a 15% reduction in carrying costs and improved cash flow. In another instance, a manufacturing company used data insights to enhance operational efficiency. By monitoring production metrics in real-time, they identified bottlenecks in their assembly line and made targeted improvements. The result was a 20% increase in production speed and significant cost savings. These examples highlight how data analytics can transform businesses, driving cost optimization and enhancing profitability.

Textual Element: Reflection Section - Evaluating Your Data Strategy

Take a moment to reflect on your current use of data analytics. Are there areas in your business where data could provide valuable insights? Consider whether your decision-making processes are truly data-driven or if there's room for improvement. This reflection section encourages you to think critically about how you can leverage data analytics to uncover cost-saving opportunities and drive your business forward.

Cloud Solutions for Cost-Effective IT Infrastructure

Imagine ditching the clunky, expensive hardware that takes up space and drains your resources. That's the promise of cloud computing. By transitioning to a cloud-based IT infrastructure, you unlock significant cost benefits. One of the most appealing aspects is scalability. Cloud services allow you to scale your IT resources up or down based on demand, much like a thermostat that adjusts to your comfort level. This flexibility means you're only paying for what you use, reducing waste and optimizing costs. Additionally, cloud computing slashes the expenses tied to maintaining on-premises hardware. Say goodbye to the days of frequent hardware upgrades and maintenance. Your cloud provider takes care of that, freeing up capital for more strategic investments.

Exploring the various cloud service models helps you choose the right fit for your business needs. Infrastructure as a Service (IaaS) offers virtualized computing resources over the internet. Think of it as renting a virtual server instead of buying a physical one. This model is perfect for businesses needing control over their hardware without the associated costs. Platform as a Service (PaaS) provides a platform allowing developers to build applications without worrying about the underlying infrastructure. It's the equivalent of renting a fully equipped kitchen to experiment with new recipes. Software as a Service (SaaS) delivers applications over the internet, eliminating the need for installations and updates. It's like having access to a digital library where the books are always up-to-date. Each model offers unique advantages, catering to different business objectives and technical requirements.

Migrating to the cloud requires a strategic approach to ensure minimal disruption. Start with a robust data migration plan. This blueprint outlines the steps to transfer your data securely and efficiently. It's like packing for a move—you want to ensure nothing gets lost in transit. Selecting the right vendor is another critical step. Look for a partner that aligns with your business goals and offers the support you need. A good vendor is like a reliable moving company, ensuring your transition is smooth and stress-free. Establishing a strong partnership with your vendor fosters collaboration and ensures ongoing support throughout the migration process. With careful planning and the right partner, cloud migration can be a seamless experience.

Once you're in the cloud, it's vital to monitor and optimize your costs. Usage monitoring and cost analytics provide insights into your consumption patterns, helping you identify areas for improvement. It's akin to checking your utility bill and realizing you can save by turning off unused lights. Rightsizing your cloud resources is another strategy to manage costs effectively. This involves adjusting your resources to match your actual usage, preventing overspending. It's like only heating the rooms you're using instead of the entire house. By staying vigilant and proactive, you can ensure that your cloud infrastructure remains cost-effective and aligned with your business needs.

Cloud computing represents a significant shift in how businesses manage IT infrastructure. By embracing the cloud, you gain access to a flexible, scalable, and cost-effective solution that supports growth and innovation. Whether you're a financial manager looking to optimize budgets, a C-suite executive seeking strategic solutions, or an operations manager aiming to streamline processes, cloud computing offers a pathway to enhanced efficiency and profitability. As you explore the potential of cloud solutions, consider how they align with your business objectives and how they can transform your IT landscape. With the right approach, cloud computing can become a powerful tool in your cost management arsenal, driving success in an ever-evolving business environment.

Adopting Agile Methodologies for Enhanced Efficiency

Agile methodologies have revolutionized the way businesses operate, offering a dynamic approach that prioritizes responsiveness and adaptability. At the heart of agile is the concept of iterative development cycles. This means breaking down projects into smaller, manageable chunks, allowing teams to deliver work in stages and make adjustments based on real-world feedback. Instead of waiting for a perfect final product, you can release functional versions early and improve them over time. This iterative process not only reduces the risk of costly mistakes but also enhances cost efficiency by ensuring resources are invested in what truly matters.

Customer feedback plays a crucial role in agile methodologies, acting as the compass that guides development. By actively seeking input from customers throughout the project, you can ensure that the end product meets their needs and expectations. This emphasis on customer collaboration not only improves satisfaction but also reduces the likelihood of expensive revisions down the line. Imagine a scenario where a product is developed without customer input, only to find it doesn't meet market demands. Agile avoids this pitfall by integrating feedback into every stage, ensuring that resources are used effectively and projects remain aligned with business goals.

Incorporating agile practices into various business functions can transform how teams collaborate and deliver results. Cross-functional agile teams bring together individuals from different departments, each contributing their expertise to achieve common objectives. This collaborative approach breaks down silos, fostering a culture of innovation and efficiency. Agile project management tools, like Jira or Trello, facilitate this process by providing a centralized platform for tracking progress, assigning tasks, and managing timelines. These tools offer a real-time view of project status, enabling teams to make informed decisions and address challenges as they arise.

The impact of agile on cost management is significant. By focusing on iterative development and customer feedback, agile methodologies help reduce project waste and optimize resource use. Teams can quickly identify and rectify issues, preventing unnecessary expenditure on unproductive activities. Furthermore, agile's emphasis on rapid iteration accelerates time-to-market, allowing businesses to capitalize on opportunities sooner. This speed is crucial in today's fast-paced market, where being first can provide a competitive edge. Agile not only enhances efficiency but also empowers organizations to respond swiftly to changing conditions, ensuring they remain relevant and profitable.

Several organizations have successfully adopted agile methodologies, reaping the benefits of enhanced efficiency and cost savings. In software development, agile transformation has become a standard, with companies like Spotify and Microsoft using agile principles to deliver innovative products quickly. These organizations have embraced agile's flexibility, allowing them to adapt to market demands and customer feedback seamlessly. Similarly, agile principles have made their way into marketing campaigns, where rapid iteration and customer engagement are key to success. Brands like Coca-Cola and IBM have leveraged agile strategies to create marketing campaigns that resonate with audiences, delivering impactful messages that drive engagement and growth. The success of these companies illustrates the transformative power of agile methodologies, highlighting their potential to revolutionize how businesses operate and achieve their goals.

Cybersecurity: Protecting Your Business Without Breaking the Bank

53

In the digital age, safeguarding your business from cyber threats is as crucial as locking your front door at night. But robust cybersecurity doesn't have to mean emptying your coffers. Start with the basics: implementing fundamental security protocols can go a long way in protecting your data. Simple steps like setting strong passwords, regularly updating software, and utilizing two-factor authentication are cost-effective yet powerful measures. These protocols act as the first line of defense, deterring many would-be intruders from gaining access to your sensitive information. Think of it like having a sturdy lock on your door—simple, yet highly effective.

Training your employees in cybersecurity is another wise investment. Often, the human element is the weakest link in the security chain. Phishing attacks and social engineering tactics prey on unsuspecting employees, tricking them into revealing confidential information. Regular training sessions can equip your team with the knowledge to recognize and thwart these threats. By fostering a culture of vigilance and awareness, you empower your staff to become active participants in maintaining your company's security. It's like teaching everyone in your household to recognize a scam phone call—knowledge is power, and it can prevent costly mistakes.

Despite best efforts, threats like ransomware continue to loom large. These attacks can lock down your systems, demanding hefty sums to restore access. To combat this, a layered security approach is key. Firewalls and intrusion detection systems form a protective barrier, monitoring and blocking suspicious activity. Endpoint security solutions further reinforce this defense, safeguarding individual devices from potential breaches. By combining these measures, you create a robust security architecture that makes it significantly harder for cybercriminals to penetrate. It's akin to having a multi-layered defense system around your home, where each layer adds an extra level of security.

Consider the example of a small business that successfully implemented budget-friendly cybersecurity measures. With limited resources, they focused on strengthening their basic security protocols and conducting regular employee training. They also invested in a cost-effective intrusion detection system that alerted them to potential threats in real-time. As a result, they were able to prevent several attacks and maintain the integrity of their data. Similarly, a non-profit organization adopted a layered security approach and partnered with a cybersecurity firm for periodic assessments. This proactive strategy ensured they remained protected while keeping costs manageable. These examples demonstrate that with strategic planning and a focus on essentials, even businesses with limited budgets can achieve strong cybersecurity protection.

Embracing Disruptive Innovations for Strategic Advantage

Disruptive innovations often redefine the rules of the game, shaking up industries by introducing groundbreaking products or services that challenge the status quo. These innovations typically start by targeting niche markets or underserved segments, gradually improving until they outperform established offerings. Think of them as the underdogs that rise to reshape entire industries. Disruptive technologies often possess characteristics like affordability, simplicity, and accessibility, making them highly attractive to consumers. Consider how digital photography displaced film cameras by offering convenience and instant results. Such disruptions can dismantle traditional business practices, forcing companies to reevaluate their strategies or risk becoming obsolete.

Spotting potential disruptive innovations in your industry requires a keen eye for emerging trends and a willingness to embrace change. You must stay informed about industry-specific innovation trends and emerging technologies with disruptive potential. For instance, in the healthcare sector, wearable devices are gaining traction, offering real-time health monitoring and personalized insights. Similarly, in the automotive industry, electric and autonomous vehicles are revolutionizing transportation. Keeping your finger on the pulse of these trends can help you anticipate shifts that could reshape your business landscape. By identifying these innovations early, you position your business to leverage them for competitive advantage.

Integrating disruptive innovations into your business strategy involves more than just recognizing their potential. It requires strategic partnerships with innovators and investment in research and development. Collaborating with startups or tech firms at the forefront of innovation can provide valuable insights and access to cutting-edge technologies. These partnerships can serve as a bridge, allowing you to incorporate disruptive elements into your operations without reinventing the wheel. Additionally, allocating resources to R&D fosters a culture of innovation within your organization. Encouraging teams to experiment and explore new ideas prepares your business to adapt swiftly to changing market conditions. It's about creating an environment where innovation is not just welcomed but actively pursued.

Consider the automotive industry, where companies like Tesla have embraced disruptive innovations to create a competitive edge. By focusing on electric vehicles and autonomous driving technologies, Tesla challenged traditional automakers and set new standards for efficiency and sustainability. The result is a brand that not only leads in innovation but also reaps the rewards of being an early adopter. Similarly, the retail sector has seen significant evolution through disruptive business models. Companies like Amazon have reshaped the landscape by leveraging e-commerce and logistics innovations, offering unprecedented convenience and choice to consumers. These examples illustrate the transformative power of embracing disruption, showcasing how businesses can achieve remarkable success by staying ahead of the curve.

Visual Element: Innovation Trend Map

Here's a quick activity to help you spot disruptive innovations: create an innovation trend map for your industry. Start by identifying key trends and technologies that are gaining momentum. Map out how these trends could impact your business and explore opportunities to integrate them into your strategy. This exercise encourages proactive thinking and helps you stay attuned to potential disruptions in your field.

As we wrap up this chapter, it's clear that embracing disruptive innovations can transform your business, offering new paths to growth and success. By staying informed, partnering strategically, and fostering a culture of innovation, you prepare your organization to thrive amidst change. In the next chapter, we'll explore how human resources and cultural change play a vital role in supporting these strategic shifts, ensuring your team is ready to embrace the future with confidence.

NOTES:

Chapter 6: Human Resources and Cultural Change

In the world of business, where numbers and strategies often take center stage, it's easy to forget the human element that truly drives success. But let's face it—behind every budget, every strategy, and every goal, there are people. Engaging these people, your employees, in cost-saving initiatives is not just a nice-to-have; it's a necessity. Imagine a sports team where every player understands the game plan and feels invested in the outcome. This shared sense of purpose is what propels the team to victory. Similarly, when employees are engaged in cost-saving efforts, they bring a level of creativity and commitment that can turn a good plan into a great one. The key is to foster an environment where they feel valued and empowered to contribute.

Engaging Employees in Cost-Saving Initiatives

Involving employees in cost-saving initiatives is like watering a plant to keep it healthy and growing. When employees feel engaged, their morale and sense of ownership soar. It's not just about cutting costs—it's about building a culture where every team member feels like they have a stake in the company's success. This sense of ownership encourages employees to think outside the box, finding innovative solutions to everyday challenges. Imagine a warehouse team that, instead of just following orders, actively seeks out ways to optimize storage and reduce waste. Their involvement not only cuts costs but also boosts efficiency and productivity. High morale and ownership translate to a more motivated workforce, ready to tackle challenges head-on.

To effectively engage employees in cost-saving goals, clear and open communication is essential. Regular team meetings serve as the backbone of this strategy, providing a platform for discussing goals, sharing progress, and addressing any concerns. Think of these meetings as a mini rally, where everyone comes together to align on the game plan and cheer each other on. Transparent updates on cost-saving progress help maintain momentum and ensure everyone is on the same page. When employees understand how their efforts contribute to the bigger picture, they feel more motivated to continue pushing forward. It's like seeing the scoreboard in a game—knowing where you stand helps guide your next move.

Creating avenues for employee feedback is another crucial aspect of engagement. Suggestion boxes or digital platforms offer a space for employees to share their ideas and feedback on cost-saving measures. This open-door policy encourages employees to speak up, knowing their voices are heard and valued. Workshops for brainstorming cost-saving ideas take this a step further, fostering a collaborative environment where employees can bounce ideas off each other and develop creative solutions. Picture a brainstorming session where a simple idea sparks a chain reaction, leading to a breakthrough that saves the company thousands. By actively involving employees in the process, you tap into a wealth of knowledge and experience that might otherwise go untapped.

Recognizing and rewarding employee contributions is the final piece of the engagement puzzle. Implementing systems like Employee of the Month programs or financial incentives for implemented ideas can make a significant impact. These programs highlight the importance of individual contributions, celebrating achievements and encouraging others to follow suit. Imagine the sense of pride an employee feels when their innovative idea is not only implemented but also rewarded. This recognition not only boosts morale but also reinforces the value of proactive thinking and collaboration. It's a win-win situation that benefits both the employees and the company.

Visual Element: Employee Engagement Infographic

To help visualize these concepts, consider an infographic illustrating the key steps in engaging employees in cost-saving initiatives. This visual aid could include icons representing regular team meetings, feedback platforms, and recognition programs, providing a clear and concise overview of the engagement process. Use this infographic as a reference to ensure you're covering all the bases in your engagement strategy, keeping employees motivated and invested in the company's success.

Training and Development: Investing in Human Capital

When it comes to cost management, training and development might not be the first thing that springs to mind. However, investing in your team's skills can yield significant cost savings. Think of training as equipping your employees with the tools they need to work smarter, not harder. By enhancing their skill sets, you empower them to perform tasks more efficiently, reducing the time and resources needed to get the job done. This, in turn, leads to fewer errors and less rework, which can be a significant drain on resources. Upskilling your team transforms them into a powerhouse of productivity and precision, directly impacting your bottom line.

Identifying the key areas for training and development is crucial for maximizing these benefits. Process improvement methodologies, such as Lean or Six Sigma, provide employees with the knowledge to streamline operations, eliminating waste and boosting efficiency. Think of these methodologies as the blueprint for a more organized and effective workplace. Meanwhile, offering financial literacy training to non-finance staff can demystify budget management and empower them to make informed decisions that align with company goals. Imagine your marketing team understanding the financial implications of their campaigns, leading to more strategic and cost-effective choices. By focusing on these areas, you build a team that's not only skilled but also aligned with the company's financial objectives.

Implementing effective training programs requires thoughtful planning and execution. Start with a needs assessment to identify the specific training requirements of your organization. This step ensures that you're not just offering generic courses but providing targeted training that addresses real gaps and opportunities. Blended learning approaches, which combine online and in-person training, provide flexibility and accommodate different learning styles. It's like having a personal trainer who tailors workouts to your needs, ensuring you get the most out of every session. By integrating various learning methods, you create a comprehensive training program that engages employees and maximizes learning outcomes.

61

Evaluating the impact of your training initiatives is essential to gauge their effectiveness and return on investment (ROI). Pre- and post-training assessments allow you to measure the knowledge and skills gained through the program. These assessments act like progress markers, showing how far your team has come and where further improvement may be needed. Long-term performance tracking takes this a step further, providing insights into how training translates into real-world results. It's about looking at the bigger picture and understanding how training impacts productivity, efficiency, and cost savings over time. By continuously evaluating your training programs, you ensure they remain relevant and impactful, driving ongoing improvements in cost management and overall performance.

With these strategies in place, you can transform training from an expense into a strategic investment that delivers tangible benefits. By focusing on the right areas, implementing effective programs, and evaluating their impact, you build a team that's equipped to tackle challenges, drive efficiency, and contribute to the company's financial success. Training and development become more than just skill-building; they become a catalyst for growth and innovation, positioning your business for long-term success.

Change Management: Overcoming Resistance to Cost-Saving Measures

Navigating change in any organization is like steering a ship through a stormy sea. The waters of change are often choppy, with many employees fearing job loss or a shift in their roles as new cost-saving measures are introduced. This fear can lead to skepticism towards new strategies, and if not addressed, can turn into resistance. Employees might worry that streamlining operations could mean downsizing, or that new technology could render their skills obsolete. Such concerns are natural, yet they can undermine even the most well-planned initiatives if not acknowledged and managed with care.

Successfully managing resistance to change is crucial for any business leader. One effective strategy is to create open forums for addressing concerns. Think of these forums as town hall meetings where everyone gets a chance to voice their thoughts and fears. By providing a platform for open dialogue, you can demystify the changes and demonstrate empathy. It also helps to involve key influencers within the organization as change advocates. These are your champions who support the initiative and can sway opinions by sharing their trust and enthusiasm with peers. Engaging these influencers early in the process can help build momentum and foster a positive outlook on the changes.

Clear and effective communication is the lifeline of any successful change initiative. Highlighting success stories from other parts of the organization or industry can be incredibly persuasive. When employees see tangible evidence of the benefits, they are more likely to embrace the changes. Aligning changes with the organization's core values also strengthens buy-in. If cost-saving measures are framed as a means to ensure the company's long-term health and sustainability, they become more than just numbers—they represent a shared commitment to the organization's success. It's like rallying a community around a common cause, where every action contributes to a greater good.

Implementing change gradually can ease transitions and reduce resistance. Consider pilot programs as a way to test new initiatives on a smaller scale. This approach allows for adjustments based on feedback before a full-scale rollout. It's similar to dipping a toe in the water before diving in, ensuring the temperature is just right. Incremental rollouts with feedback loops enable continuous learning and adaptation. As you gather feedback, you refine the process, making the change more palatable and effective. This iterative approach not only builds confidence but also creates a culture of continuous improvement, where change is seen as an opportunity rather than a threat.

By focusing on these strategies, you can transform potential resistance into acceptance and enthusiasm. It's about creating an environment where change is embraced and everyone feels part of the journey. Through empathy, communication, and gradual implementation, you guide your team through the storm, emerging stronger and more united on the other side. Change management, when done right, can be a powerful catalyst for growth and innovation, ensuring that your cost-saving measures are not just implemented but thrive within your organization.

The Impact of Employee Engagement on Operational Efficiency

Employee engagement is like the hidden engine of operational efficiency, quietly driving productivity and reducing turnover. When employees feel engaged, they bring their best selves to work, leading to higher productivity levels. Imagine an assembly line where each worker not only understands their role but also takes pride in it. This sense of ownership leads to fewer mistakes and a smoother workflow. Engaged employees are also less likely to call in sick or leave for greener pastures, reducing absenteeism and turnover. This stability is crucial for maintaining momentum and ensuring that operations run like a well-oiled machine.

Several factors work together to boost employee engagement and, in turn, improve efficiency. Recognition and appreciation are at the heart of engagement. When employees know their efforts are valued, they're more likely to go the extra mile. Imagine receiving a heartfelt thank-you from your boss after completing a challenging project. That acknowledgment can make all the difference. Opportunities for career growth are another powerful motivator. Employees who see a path for advancement within the company are more likely to invest their time and energy into their work. They're not just clocking in and out—they're building a future with the organization.

To truly understand and enhance engagement, it's essential to measure it. Employee engagement surveys provide valuable insights into how employees feel about their roles, their teams, and the company as a whole. These surveys act as a barometer, helping you identify areas for improvement and celebrate areas of strength. But surveys alone aren't enough. Performance metrics analysis complements these insights by showing how engagement translates into tangible outcomes, such as productivity and efficiency. By analyzing these metrics, you can make informed decisions about where to focus your engagement efforts for maximum impact.

Boosting engagement requires more than just understanding it; actionable strategies are key. Team-building activities can help foster a sense of camaraderie and collaboration among employees. These activities break down barriers and encourage open communication, creating a more cohesive team. Flexible work arrangements are another effective strategy. By offering employees the option to work remotely or adjust their schedules, you show that you trust them to manage their time effectively. This flexibility not only enhances work-life balance but also boosts morale, leading to a happier, more productive workforce.

Textual Element: Reflection Section - Assessing Engagement Strategies

Take a moment to reflect on your current engagement strategies. Are they effectively boosting productivity and reducing turnover? Consider conducting an employee engagement survey or analyzing performance metrics to gain insights. This reflection section offers a chance to evaluate and refine your approach, ensuring that your strategies align with your goals for enhanced operational efficiency. By continually assessing and adjusting your strategies, you create a dynamic environment where engagement thrives, driving success across the organization.

6.5 Building a Culture of Continuous Improvement

Imagine for a moment that your business is a living organism. To thrive, it must continuously adapt, grow, and evolve. This is the essence of a culture of continuous improvement, where change isn't feared but embraced as a constant. When you foster such a culture, you encourage innovation and creativity to flourish, turning challenges into opportunities for growth. Picture a team that views setbacks not as roadblocks but as stepping stones to better solutions. This mindset transforms the workplace into a dynamic environment where every employee feels empowered to contribute to ongoing enhancements. It's about creating a space where ideas are valued, and innovation is woven into the fabric of everyday operations.

To support continuous improvement, you need robust frameworks that guide efforts and maintain momentum. The PDCA (Plan-Do-Check-Act) cycle offers a structured approach to problem-solving, driving improvements in a systematic way. It begins with planning, where you identify issues and devise strategies to tackle them. The doing phase involves implementing these strategies, followed by checking to evaluate their effectiveness. Finally, the act phase ensures that successful initiatives are standardized and integrated into regular practices. This cycle creates a rhythm of reflection and action, fostering an environment where improvement is an ongoing pursuit. Alongside PDCA, Kaizen events bring together teams to focus on specific processes or areas in need of enhancement. These events are like concentrated bursts of creativity, where employees collaborate to brainstorm and implement solutions. Through these structured approaches, continuous improvement becomes not just an initiative but a core element of your organizational culture.

Collaboration is the heartbeat of continuous improvement. When cross-departmental teams come together, they bring diverse perspectives that enrich problem-solving efforts. Imagine a room filled with colleagues from sales, operations, and finance, each contributing their unique insights to a shared goal. This diversity of thought sparks creativity, leading to innovative solutions that might not have emerged in isolation. By fostering cross-departmental improvement teams, you break down silos and promote a culture of shared goals and objectives. These teams work towards a common vision, aligning their efforts to drive meaningful change across the organization. It's about creating a tapestry of collaboration where each thread strengthens the whole.

Recognizing achievements in continuous improvement is crucial for maintaining engagement and motivation. When teams and individuals see their efforts acknowledged, it reinforces the value of their contributions and encourages further involvement. Consider implementing continuous improvement awards to celebrate standout initiatives. These awards act as a spotlight, highlighting the impact of innovative solutions and inspiring others to follow suit. Public acknowledgment of successful projects also plays a vital role. Whether it's a shoutout in a company-wide meeting or a feature in the internal newsletter, this recognition fosters a sense of pride and accomplishment. It shows employees that their hard work doesn't go unnoticed and that even small improvements can lead to significant gains. By establishing recognition mechanisms, you create a culture where continuous improvement is not only encouraged but celebrated as a collective achievement.

6.6 Incentivizing Cost-Conscious Behavior Among Staff

Incentivizing cost-conscious behavior among your staff is like planting seeds that grow into a garden of efficiency and savings. When employees understand how their actions impact the bottom line and are motivated to make cost-effective decisions, they become active participants in the organization's financial well-being. Aligning individual actions with organizational goals is key. When employees see that their efforts directly contribute to the company's success, they're more likely to take ownership of cost-saving initiatives. Think of it as a team sport, where every player knows their role and how it contributes to winning the game. This alignment encourages employees to seek out proactive cost-saving measures, turning everyday tasks into opportunities for innovation and efficiency.

Developing effective incentive programs is a powerful way to promote cost-conscious behavior. Performance-based bonuses offer tangible rewards for achieving specific cost-saving targets. These bonuses act as a carrot, motivating employees to go above and beyond in their efforts to reduce expenses. Non-monetary recognition systems can also be highly effective. Whether it's a simple thank-you note or a spotlight in the company newsletter, these gestures show employees that their contributions are valued and appreciated. By creating a culture of recognition, you foster an environment where cost-consciousness becomes a natural part of the workday. It's about cultivating a mindset where employees feel empowered to make decisions that benefit both themselves and the organization.

Aligning incentives with measurable outcomes ensures that the programs are impactful and meaningful. Specific cost reduction targets provide clear benchmarks for success, helping employees understand what is expected of them. Quality improvement

67

benchmarks ensure that cost-saving efforts don't compromise the integrity of products or services. By setting these standards, you create a framework that guides employees' actions and helps them focus their efforts on achieving tangible results. It's like setting a course for a ship—clear goals ensure that everyone is steering in the same direction, working together towards a common destination.

Evaluating the success of incentive programs is crucial for understanding their impact and making necessary adjustments. Gathering feedback from participants provides insights into what works and what doesn't, helping you refine the programs over time. Analyzing cost-saving impacts offers a clear picture of the financial benefits, allowing you to measure the return on investment. This analysis acts as a compass, guiding future initiatives and ensuring that the programs continue to drive meaningful change. By continuously evaluating and adapting your incentive programs, you create a dynamic environment where cost-conscious behavior is not only encouraged but embedded in the organization's DNA.

Incentivizing Cost-Conscious Behavior Among Staff

In the landscape of modern business, incentivizing cost-conscious behavior isn't just about saving a few bucks here and there. It's about creating a mindset where every employee sees themselves as a steward of the organization's resources. Imagine a workplace where each decision—from turning off unused lights to optimizing travel expenses—is made with an eye on the bottom line. Aligning individual actions with organizational goals helps build a cohesive culture where everyone understands the impact of their choices. When employees are encouraged to actively seek out cost-saving initiatives, they become more engaged and proactive. This not only boosts morale but also encourages innovation, as team members find new ways to cut costs without sacrificing quality. By promoting cost-consciousness, organizations can create a more sustainable and financially sound future.

Developing effective incentive programs is key to nurturing this cost-conscious culture. Performance-based bonuses are a straightforward way to reward employees for meeting specific cost-saving targets.

68

These bonuses provide a tangible reward for efforts that go beyond everyday duties, encouraging employees to think creatively about how to reduce expenses. However, not every incentive needs to carry a price tag. Non-monetary recognition systems can be equally powerful. Acknowledging employees' contributions through public recognition, additional responsibilities, or opportunities for professional growth can foster a sense of accomplishment and drive. These systems help to create an environment where everyone feels valued, and their efforts to save costs are appreciated. By diversifying incentives, organizations ensure that they appeal to a wide range of motivations, making cost-conscious behavior a part of the company's DNA.

Ensuring that incentives are linked to measurable outcomes is crucial for their success. Specific cost reduction targets provide clear goals that employees can aim for, helping them to understand the direct impact of their actions. Quality improvement benchmarks ensure that the focus on cost savings doesn't lead to compromised standards. By setting these benchmarks, you maintain a balance between saving money and delivering value. It's like aiming for a target with a clear bullseye—employees know exactly what is expected and what they need to achieve. This clarity not only motivates but also guides employees in their efforts, ensuring that cost-saving measures align with the broader objectives of the organization.

To evaluate the success of incentive programs, gathering feedback from participants is essential. This feedback provides insights into what works and what doesn't, helping organizations refine their approach over time. Employees' perspectives can reveal unexpected benefits or challenges that might not be apparent from a managerial standpoint. Additionally, analyzing the cost-saving impacts offers a clear picture of the financial benefits achieved through these programs. This analysis acts as a scorecard, showing the effectiveness of different initiatives and guiding future decisions. By continuously assessing and adjusting incentive programs, organizations can ensure they remain relevant and impactful, driving meaningful change and fostering a culture of cost-consciousness.

As we wrap up this exploration of incentivizing cost-conscious behavior, it's clear that the key lies in aligning individual actions with the company's goals. By encouraging proactive initiatives and developing comprehensive incentive programs, organizations can create a culture where cost-saving becomes second nature. The next chapter will delve into the role of technology in enhancing efficiency, building on the foundation of a cost-conscious workforce to drive further innovation and growth.

NOTES:

Chapter 7: Real-World Applications and Case Studies

Every business journey is a tapestry of challenges, strategies, and triumphs. This chapter delves into the intricate world of cost management through the lens of real-world applications and case studies. Imagine a colossal manufacturing giant, a titan in its industry, but burdened with spiraling costs and efficiency woes. Let's explore how this industry leader confronted its challenges head-on and emerged stronger, leaner, and more competitive.

Case Study: Cost Reduction in a Manufacturing Giant

Our story begins with a manufacturing giant grappling with escalating production costs. High energy consumption rates drained profits like a leaky faucet, while inefficient production workflows stifled productivity and innovation. Picture factory floors sprawling with machinery, humming with activity, yet operating at less than optimal efficiency. This behemoth faced the daunting task of reinventing its operations to remain competitive in a market where every penny counts.

The company embarked on a transformative journey to tackle its challenges. They introduced energy-efficient technologies, revolutionizing how energy was consumed and managed throughout their facilities. Advanced sensors and smart systems replaced outdated machinery, slashing energy costs and reducing the carbon footprint. This move not only cut expenses but also aligned with growing consumer demand for greener practices. Simultaneously, they embraced lean manufacturing principles, meticulously analyzing each step of their production processes. The result was a streamlined operation, with waste minimized and resources optimized. By focusing on continuous improvement and employee empowerment, they cultivated an environment where efficiency thrived.

The outcomes of these initiatives were nothing short of remarkable. Operational costs plummeted, freeing up capital for reinvestment and innovation. Production efficiency soared, with output levels increasing without additional costs. This newfound efficiency translated into enhanced market competitiveness, allowing the company to offer better pricing and faster delivery times. As a bonus, the company's commitment to sustainability attracted eco-conscious consumers, broadening its market appeal.

Reflecting on their journey, the manufacturing giant gleaned invaluable lessons. Continuous monitoring and refinement of processes proved critical to maintaining gains and fostering resilience. They recognized the importance of involving employees at all levels, ensuring that everyone felt invested in the company's success. Moving forward, the company plans to maintain its focus on innovation, seeking out emerging technologies and practices that promise further efficiency gains. By keeping their finger on the pulse of industry trends and consumer expectations, they aim to remain at the forefront of their market.

Interactive Element: Reflection Section - Applying Lessons Learned

As you consider this case study, take a moment to reflect on your own operations. Are there areas where energy consumption is higher than necessary? Could your workflows benefit from a leaner approach? Use this reflection to identify potential areas for improvement. Consider gathering input from your team, encouraging them to share their insights and ideas. This collaborative approach not only uncovers hidden opportunities but also fosters a culture of continuous improvement, driving your organization toward greater efficiency and profitability.

How a Small Business Achieved Big Savings

Let's shift our focus to a small business that, despite financial constraints, managed to achieve substantial savings. Picture a local retailer operating on a shoestring budget, where every dollar counts and rising supplier costs threaten to squeeze profit margins even tighter. This small business faced the common challenge of limited financial flexibility, a situation familiar to many entrepreneurs and business owners. Supplier costs were on the rise, leaving the company scrambling to maintain affordability for their customers while preserving their own financial health. It was a delicate balancing act, one that required strategic thinking and a willingness to adapt.

To tackle these challenges head-on, the business took a multipronged approach. They started by renegotiating supplier contracts, an often-overlooked strategy that can yield significant savings. By establishing strong relationships with suppliers and demonstrating loyalty, the business was able to secure more favorable terms. This included bulk purchase discounts and extended payment periods, which eased cash flow pressures. Such negotiations require tact and a clear understanding of both parties' needs, but when done right, they strengthen partnerships and reduce costs.

Next, the business embraced digital marketing strategies, recognizing the shift in consumer behavior towards online platforms. Rather than investing heavily in traditional advertising, they focused on building a robust online presence. Social media channels and targeted email campaigns became their new storefronts, allowing them to reach a broader audience without the overhead of physical advertising. These digital tools provided valuable insights into customer preferences, enabling the business to tailor its offerings and enhance customer engagement. The cost-effectiveness of digital marketing lies in its ability to reach specific demographics with minimal expenditure, making it an invaluable asset for small businesses.

Streamlining inventory management was another critical component of their strategy. The business implemented an inventory tracking system that provided real-time data on stock levels, reducing the risk of overstocking or stockouts. This system allowed for just-in-time ordering, minimizing holding costs and freeing up capital. Better inventory control also meant they could respond more agilely to market demands, ensuring that popular items were always available and slow-movers were phased out promptly. The result was a leaner inventory that maximized sales potential and minimized waste.

The impact of these measures was transformative. Profitability margins increased as costs decreased, providing the business with much-needed financial breathing room. Enhanced cash flow management meant they could reinvest in growth opportunities, such as expanding their product line or improving customer service. The business also enjoyed a more predictable financial outlook, which boosted confidence among stakeholders and positioned them well for future challenges.

For other small businesses seeking similar successes, there are valuable lessons to be learned. Flexible budgeting is crucial, allowing businesses to adapt quickly to changing circumstances and allocate resources efficiently. This flexibility enables businesses to prioritize spending on areas that drive the most value, while cutting back on non-essential expenses. Leveraging technology is another key takeaway. By investing in tools that enhance operational efficiency and provide customer insights, small businesses can compete with larger rivals without breaking the bank. Embracing digital solutions not only saves money but also opens up new avenues for growth and innovation.

It's clear that with the right mindset and strategies, small businesses can overcome financial hurdles and thrive in competitive markets. By focusing on negotiation, digital transformation, and efficient inventory management, they can unlock savings and boost their bottom line. The success of this small business serves as a testament to the power of strategic cost management and its ability to drive financial stability and growth.

Lessons Learned from a Failed Cost-Cutting Initiative

In the complex world of business management, even the best-laid plans can go awry. Consider an organization that embarked on a cost-cutting initiative with high hopes, only to find itself facing unexpected hurdles. The underlying issue was a lack of stakeholder buy-in. Picture this: a boardroom filled with executives, each with their own vision and priorities, but no unified agreement on the direction of cost reduction. Without everyone on the same page, the initiative lacked the necessary support to drive effective change. This, coupled with insufficient planning, meant the strategies weren't fully thought through. There was a rush to implement cuts without a comprehensive understanding of potential pitfalls or the broader implications on operations. Additionally, the initiative suffered from misalignment with business goals. The cuts, though well-intentioned, didn't align with the company's long-term vision, creating a disconnect that rippled through the organization.

The fallout from this failed initiative was significant. Employees, already wary of change, grew increasingly dissatisfied. Imagine coming to work each day, unsure of how new policies might affect your role or the tools you rely on to do your job. Morale took a hit, leading to decreased productivity and increased turnover rates. Financially, the organization didn't fare much better. The haphazard cuts led to savings on paper but eroded key areas that drove revenue. The anticipated financial relief never materialized, and the company found itself grappling with losses instead. This misstep not only impacted the bottom line but also tarnished its reputation among clients and stakeholders, shaking confidence in its leadership.

Recognizing the need to course-correct, the organization took decisive steps to recover. They began with a thorough post-mortem analysis, dissecting what went wrong and why. This wasn't about pointing fingers but understanding the root causes to prevent future failures. Realigning their cost-cutting strategies with organizational objectives became a priority. It was crucial to ensure that every decision reflected the company's core values and long-term goals. This involved engaging stakeholders at all levels, from the executive suite to the shop floor, to foster a sense of ownership and collaboration. By creating a shared vision and encouraging open dialogue, the organization laid a stronger foundation for future initiatives.

From this experience, several key learnings emerged. Perhaps the most critical was the importance of stakeholder engagement. Before launching any significant initiative, it's essential to gain buy-in from those who will be affected. This means involving them in the planning process, understanding their concerns, and building consensus. Another vital lesson was the necessity for thorough risk assessment. It's easy to focus on potential savings without considering the risks involved. By evaluating what could go wrong and planning for contingencies, the organization could have better navigated the challenges it faced. These lessons serve as a poignant reminder that successful cost reduction isn't just about cutting expenses; it's about thoughtful, strategic planning that aligns with broader business objectives and considers the human element at its core.

Transformative Cost Management in the Tech Industry

Navigating cost management in the tech industry is akin to riding a roller coaster with its rapid twists and turns. Tech companies face unique challenges, like the relentless pace of technology obsolescence. Imagine releasing a cutting-edge device only to have it deemed outdated within months. This cycle demands constant innovation and reinvestment, stretching budgets and increasing financial pressure. In addition, high research and development (R&D) expenses are a constant hurdle. The pursuit of groundbreaking technologies requires significant investment in talent, equipment, and testing. Companies must balance the imperative to innovate with the need to manage these high costs effectively.

To address these financial pressures, tech companies have crafted innovative strategies. Agile development methodologies have emerged as a powerful tool, allowing teams to work in short, iterative cycles. This approach not only speeds up product development but also enhances flexibility, enabling rapid responses to market changes. Teams can pivot quickly, adapting to new information or shifting consumer demands without incurring significant costs. Meanwhile, the adoption of open-source technologies has been a game-changer. By leveraging community-driven software, companies can reduce licensing fees and development costs. Open-source platforms foster collaboration and innovation, providing a fertile ground for new ideas without the hefty price tag of proprietary solutions.

These strategies have proven highly effective in achieving financial goals. Agile methodologies have led to accelerated product development cycles, allowing companies to bring new products to market faster than ever before. This speed not only enhances competitiveness but also maximizes return on investment by reducing time-to-market. Optimized resource allocation, a hallmark of agile practices, ensures that resources are directed where they are most needed, minimizing waste and maximizing impact. The use of open-source technologies has also resulted in substantial savings, freeing up funds for further innovation. By reducing reliance on costly proprietary systems, tech companies can reinvest in R&D, driving future growth and maintaining their technological edge.

Insights from tech companies across the industry highlight the importance of collaborative innovation ecosystems. These ecosystems, where companies, startups, and academic institutions collaborate, create a dynamic environment for sharing knowledge and resources. By pooling expertise and infrastructure, participants can tackle complex challenges more efficiently, reducing costs and accelerating innovation. Strategic partnerships for cost-sharing further enhance this collaborative approach. By partnering with other companies, tech firms can share the financial burden of R&D, reducing individual costs while benefiting from shared insights and discoveries. These partnerships also foster a culture of open innovation, where ideas flow freely and collaboration leads to breakthroughs that would be difficult to achieve independently.

The tech industry's approach to cost management offers valuable lessons for businesses across sectors. The focus on agility, open-source solutions, and collaboration highlights the importance of flexibility and innovation in cost management. By embracing these strategies, companies can navigate financial challenges with greater ease and position themselves for long-term success. As technology continues to evolve, the ability to adapt and innovate will remain crucial, driving both cost efficiency and competitive advantage.

Strategic Cost Reduction in the Service Sector

Picture the bustling service sector, where the rhythm of customer interactions and labor-intensive operations creates a unique set of financial challenges. Unlike industries with tangible goods, service-oriented businesses often grapple with fluctuating demand cycles. One moment, the demand could be sky-high, and the next, it could drop, leaving businesses scrambling to adjust. This unpredictability makes it crucial to maintain a flexible workforce. Labor costs can swell during peak periods, putting pressure on margins. For a business like a call center, staffing must be nimble, able to expand or contract based on customer call volumes. It's a constant juggling act, balancing quality service with financial feasibility.

In response to these challenges, service companies have turned to strategic cost-reduction methods, focusing on flexible staffing models and process automation. By implementing flexible staffing, businesses can adapt to demand fluctuations without being overburdened by fixed labor costs. This approach often involves employing part-time workers or freelancers who can be called upon when needed. It's like having a pool of expert lifeguards ready to jump in when the waves get high. Such a strategy not only saves money but also ensures that customer service remains robust, even during peak times. In tandem, process automation plays a vital role in reducing repetitive tasks, freeing up human resources for more valuable interactions. Think of a hotel chain using automated check-in kiosks to handle routine bookings, allowing staff to focus on creating memorable guest experiences.

The impact of these strategic cost reductions is palpable. Improved customer satisfaction scores often follow, as businesses can maintain high service levels without the strain of overstaffing. Profit margins see a healthy boost when labor costs are optimized, and tasks are automated, cutting down on inefficiency. It's like trimming a tree to allow it to grow taller and stronger. By doing more with less, service businesses find themselves more agile, better positioned to respond to market demands, and more competitive in their offerings. The marriage of technology and strategic planning creates a service ecosystem where quality and efficiency coexist harmoniously.

Across the sector, trends and innovations are shaping the future of cost management. The growing use of artificial intelligence (AI) in customer interactions is a game-changer. AI-powered chatbots and virtual assistants handle basic queries, providing quick solutions and freeing staff to tackle more complex issues. This technology not only reduces labor costs but also enhances customer satisfaction by delivering instant support. Moreover, the adoption of subscription-based service models offers a steady revenue stream, mitigating the risks associated with demand volatility. Consider a fitness center offering monthly memberships, ensuring a consistent cash flow regardless of seasonal attendance fluctuations. These models allow businesses to plan with greater financial certainty, building resilience against the ebbs and flows of customer demand.

Service businesses are embracing these innovations, weaving them into their operational fabric to drive efficiency and growth. The application of AI and the strategic restructuring of pricing models exemplify the sector's adaptability and forward-thinking approach. As these trends continue to evolve, they promise to redefine how service companies manage costs, paving the way for a new era of smart, sustainable business practices. By harnessing the power of technology and strategic flexibility, the service sector can navigate its unique challenges with confidence, ensuring that businesses remain profitable and customer-focused.

Cross-Industry Insights for Effective Cost Management

In the world of business, regardless of your industry or niche, certain cost management challenges seem universal. Rising material costs, for instance, have become a significant concern across sectors. Whether you're in manufacturing, technology, or retail, the increasing prices of raw materials can eat into your profit margins. It's like trying to fill a basket with water—no matter how fast you pour, the gaps let your profits slip away. Then there's the ever-present burden of regulatory compliance expenses. As governments tighten rules around sustainability, data privacy, and labor practices, companies find themselves spending more time and money to stay compliant. These costs, although necessary, can feel like a tax on innovation, diverting resources from growth-focused initiatives.

But with challenges come opportunities, and many businesses have turned to successful cross-industry cost management practices to navigate these turbulent waters. One approach, inspired by sectors from automotive to healthcare, is the application of lean management principles. By systematically identifying and eliminating waste, companies can operate more efficiently and reduce costs across the board. Lean management isn't just about cutting corners; it's about creating value by doing more with less. Imagine a restaurant that streamlines its menu and optimizes kitchen processes, reducing wait times and improving customer satisfaction while cutting costs.

Strategic outsourcing partnerships also offer a pathway to cost efficiency. By collaborating with third-party providers, businesses can access specialized skills and resources without the overhead of maintaining those capabilities in-house. This is like choosing to rent a high-end camera for a specific project instead of buying one outright. Many industries, from finance to logistics, have successfully leveraged outsourcing to enhance their competitiveness and agility. It's about focusing on core competencies and letting experts handle the rest, ensuring that every dollar spent delivers maximum value.

The benefits of cross-industry learning are vast and varied. When businesses look beyond their immediate sector, they gain fresh perspectives that can spark innovation and drive change. Think of it as a cross-pollination of ideas, where a technique perfected in one industry finds new life and application in another. This transfer of skills and techniques can lead to breakthroughs that might otherwise be missed. For instance, a tech company might learn from agriculture's precision farming techniques to improve its data analytics processes, or a retail chain might adopt hospitality's customer engagement strategies to enhance the shopping experience.

For businesses seeking practical insights, there are several actionable takeaways that apply across industries. First, the importance of benchmarking against industry leaders cannot be overstated. By analyzing the practices of top performers, companies can identify areas for improvement and set realistic targets. It's like aspiring athletes studying the techniques of champions to hone their own skills. Continuous improvement should also be a cultural norm, not just a one-off exercise. By fostering an environment where employees are encouraged to seek out efficiencies and challenge the status quo, businesses can maintain a competitive edge. This involves regular training, open communication channels, and a willingness to adapt to new methods and technologies.

In the end, effective cost management is about more than just cutting expenses. It's about creating a resilient, adaptable organization that can

80

thrive in the face of challenges. By looking beyond traditional boundaries and embracing lessons from other industries, companies can develop strategies that not only save money but also unlock new opportunities for growth. As we explore these themes further, keep in mind that the most successful businesses are those that remain open to learning and ready to innovate, no matter where the inspiration comes from.

NOTES:

Chapter 8: Measuring Success and Ensuring Sustainability

In the ever-evolving landscape of business, understanding the impact of your cost-saving initiatives is akin to having a compass on a long journey. Without it, you may find yourself wandering off course, despite your best intentions. Imagine a flourishing garden; to keep it thriving, you must regularly check which plants are growing well and which need more attention. Similarly, evaluating the effectiveness of your cost-saving measures ensures that your business efforts are bearing fruit and not merely sprouting weeds. Let's delve into how you can systematically assess these initiatives and steer your organization towards sustainable success.

Evaluating the Impact of Cost-Saving Initiatives

To measure the success of your cost-saving initiatives, developing specific metrics is crucial. These metrics act as your yardstick, allowing you to gauge the effectiveness of your efforts. Among the most telling indicators is the cost reduction percentage, which shows how much you've managed to save against your initial expenses. Improvement in profit margins is another vital metric; it's not just about cutting costs, but also how these reductions translate into increased profitability. By keeping a close eye on these numbers, you not only track progress but also motivate your team by showcasing tangible results of their hard work.

Once you've implemented your cost-saving strategies, conducting post-implementation reviews is the next step. These reviews are a chance to take a step back and evaluate the overall performance of your initiatives. Gather feedback from stakeholders, including team members and partners, to understand their perspectives on the changes. This feedback provides invaluable insights into what's working and what needs tweaking. Additionally, analyze any deviations from expected outcomes. If a particular initiative fell short of its goals, understanding why it happened is critical. Was there a misalignment in execution, or did external factors play a role? This analysis helps refine your strategies, ensuring they are more effective in the future.

Beyond financial metrics, it's essential to consider the broader impact of your cost-saving efforts on both financial health and operational efficiency. Have these initiatives reduced operational bottlenecks, allowing your team to work more smoothly? Increased resource utilization rates are another indicator of success. Are you getting more output from the same resources? These operational improvements are often as valuable as financial gains, contributing to a more streamlined and agile organization. By evaluating these aspects, you ensure that cost-saving measures enhance the overall efficiency of your business, not just the bottom line.

Textual Element: Case Study - Evaluating Success in Cost Reduction

Take, for example, a retail company that undertook a comprehensive cost-saving initiative. By renegotiating supplier contracts and optimizing inventory management, they achieved a 15% reduction in costs. In their post-implementation review, feedback from store managers highlighted improved stock availability and customer satisfaction. Analyzing financial data revealed an 8% increase in profit margins, with reduced waste contributing to a leaner operation. On the other hand, in the manufacturing sector, a company focused on automation and energy efficiency. Their initiatives led to a 20% decrease in production costs. Feedback from the production floor indicated smoother workflows and fewer interruptions, enhancing overall productivity. These case studies illustrate how businesses across sectors can successfully evaluate and refine their cost-saving strategies, ensuring they align with broader business objectives.

By embracing these evaluation practices, you gain a comprehensive understanding of your cost-saving initiatives' impact, empowering you to make informed decisions and drive sustainable success.

Sustainability in Cost Management: Long-Term Strategies

In today's business climate, sustainability in cost management goes far beyond just keeping expenses low. It's about creating a resilient financial plan that can withstand the test of time and market fluctuations. Imagine a structure built not just with speed in mind but designed to last for decades. Avoiding short-term fixes is crucial, as they might offer immediate relief but rarely lead to lasting success. Instead, integrating long-term cost-saving measures ensures stability and growth. Resilience in financial planning means having the foresight to anticipate changes and challenges, allowing you to adapt without losing ground. Just like a seasoned sailor navigates turbulent waters with a steady hand and a well-prepared ship, your business needs a robust strategy to manage costs sustainably.

Sustainable cost management practices are the cornerstone of this long-term approach. Lifecycle cost analysis is an essential practice that considers the total cost of ownership, from acquisition to disposal. This perspective helps you make informed decisions that align with both your financial goals and sustainability commitments. For instance, investing in energy-efficient equipment may have a higher upfront cost but can lead to significant savings over time. Sustainable procurement practices also play a pivotal role. By sourcing materials responsibly and fostering strong relationships with suppliers who share your values, you not only reduce costs but also support an ethical supply chain. These practices ensure that your organization remains competitive while contributing positively to the world around you.

Embedding sustainability into your company's culture is perhaps the most effective way to ensure these practices take root. This cultural shift requires commitment at all levels, starting with employee training on sustainability principles. When employees understand the impact of their actions, they're more likely to embrace cost-saving measures that align with sustainability goals. Leadership plays a crucial role, too. A commitment from the top sets the tone for the entire organization, signaling that sustainability is not just a buzzword but a core value. Leaders who walk the talk inspire their teams to follow suit, fostering an environment where sustainable practices are second nature.

85

Structured frameworks provide a roadmap for achieving sustainability in cost management. The triple bottom line framework is one such approach, measuring success not just in terms of profit but also considering social and environmental impacts. This holistic view encourages businesses to balance financial goals with broader societal responsibilities. Circular economy principles also offer valuable insights. By designing processes that eliminate waste and promote the continuous use of resources, businesses can realize significant cost savings while reducing their environmental footprint. These frameworks guide organizations in making strategic decisions that align with both short-term objectives and long-term sustainability.

To wrap up, sustainability in cost management is not just about cutting costs; it's about building a resilient, responsible organization that thrives over the long haul. By adopting sustainable practices, integrating them into your culture, and leveraging structured frameworks, you position your business for enduring success. This approach not only enhances your bottom line but also contributes to a more sustainable future for all.

Adjusting Strategies Based on Performance Metrics

In the complex world of cost management, performance metrics act like signposts, guiding you toward strategic adjustments that refine your approach and drive success. Imagine you're on a road trip. Performance metrics are the GPS directions that help you navigate twists and turns. Key Performance Indicators (KPIs) play a crucial role in this journey, offering continuous insights that fuel data-driven decision-making. By tracking these KPIs, you ensure that your cost-saving strategies remain relevant and effective, adapting to changing business landscapes. Whether it's keeping a close eye on resource utilization rates or monitoring operational efficiency, these metrics provide the clarity needed to make informed adjustments. Through this lens, you can identify what's working, what's not, and where to steer your efforts next.

Regular strategy reviews are vital in keeping your cost-saving efforts on track. Think of these reviews as routine maintenance checks for your car, ensuring everything runs smoothly. Quarterly performance assessment meetings offer a structured opportunity to evaluate your strategies, gathering insights from various stakeholders. These meetings encourage open dialogue, where team members can share observations and insights. Strategic review workshops take this a step further, providing a collaborative space to brainstorm and refine strategies. By fostering an environment of continuous evaluation, you keep your strategies fresh and aligned with business objectives. This proactive approach ensures that your cost management efforts remain agile, ready to adapt to new challenges and opportunities as they arise.

A culture of adaptability is the backbone of successful strategic adjustment. In a world where change is constant, fostering a culture that embraces flexibility is key. Encouraging innovative thinking within your organization empowers employees to explore new avenues and challenge the status quo. Rewarding adaptability in strategy execution promotes a mindset that values change and sees it as an opportunity for growth. By nurturing this culture, you create an organization that thrives on innovation and resilience. It's about empowering your team to think outside the box, experiment with new ideas, and embrace change as a catalyst for improvement. This cultural shift transforms how your organization approaches cost management, making it a dynamic and forward-thinking entity.

Real-world examples highlight the power of strategic adjustments based on performance metrics. Consider a tech company that successfully adapted its pricing strategy in response to market insights. By closely monitoring customer demand trends and competitor pricing, the company identified an opportunity to adjust its pricing model. This strategic shift not only increased market share but also enhanced profitability. Similarly, in the service industry, a company leveraged performance data to adjust its offerings in response to changing customer preferences. By analyzing feedback and usage patterns, the company introduced tailored services that better aligned with customer needs, resulting in increased customer satisfaction and loyalty. These examples underscore the importance of using performance metrics as a foundation for strategic adjustments, enabling businesses to remain competitive and responsive in an ever-changing landscape.

Ensuring Alignment with Strategic Business Goals

Aligning cost-saving efforts with your overarching business goals is like making sure all the gears in a machine are turning together smoothly. When cost management strategies are in sync with your strategic objectives, you create a synergy that enhances strategic coherence and maximizes resource allocation efficiency. Imagine a car engine where every part works in harmony; you get better performance and fuel efficiency. Similarly, when your cost-saving initiatives align with your business goals, you not only save money but also ensure that those savings propel you closer to your vision. This alignment allows for a more streamlined operation where resources are allocated precisely where they're needed most, cutting down on waste and boosting efficiency across the board.

To achieve this level of alignment, developing frameworks and tools is crucial. The balanced scorecard is one such tool that helps organizations translate their vision and strategy into tangible actions. It provides a comprehensive view of organizational performance by linking financial and non-financial metrics. Think of it as a dashboard for your business, giving you insights into various areas like finance, customer relations, internal processes, and learning and growth. Similarly, strategic alignment matrices offer a visual representation of how your cost-saving initiatives support your strategic goals. These tools provide a structured approach to ensuring that every action you take contributes to the bigger picture, helping you stay on track and measure progress effectively.

Facilitating cross-departmental alignment sessions is another vital step in ensuring that everyone in the organization is on the same page. Cross-functional strategy alignment workshops bring together representatives from different departments to collaborate on aligning their efforts with the company's strategic objectives. Imagine a team of musicians coming together to rehearse a piece of music. Each one plays a different instrument, but together they create a harmonious symphony. Similarly, joint goal-setting initiatives encourage departments to work together towards common goals, fostering a sense of unity and shared purpose. By breaking down silos and encouraging open communication, these sessions promote collaboration and ensure that cost-saving efforts are aligned across the organization.

The impact of alignment on business success is profound. When your cost-saving strategies are aligned with your strategic business goals, you're more likely to see an increased return on investment (ROI) from your initiatives. Aligned efforts ensure that resources are used efficiently, leading to higher productivity and profitability. Moreover, this alignment improves stakeholder satisfaction. When stakeholders see that the organization is committed to achieving its strategic objectives through prudent cost management, their confidence in the business grows. This confidence translates into stronger relationships with investors, customers, and employees, all of whom play a vital role in driving the organization's success.

Continuous Monitoring and Improvement Processes

In the fast-paced world of business, continuous monitoring is like having a vigilant lookout on a ship, always scanning the horizon for changes. It's crucial for maintaining the effectiveness of your cost management strategies. By engaging in real-time data analysis, you gain immediate insights into your financial landscape, allowing you to make informed decisions on the fly. Think of it as having a live dashboard that displays your current financial health, helping you spot trends, anomalies, and areas needing attention. Continuous feedback loops add another layer of depth to this process. By consistently gathering input from various departments, you create a dynamic system that adjusts and evolves, ensuring your strategies remain relevant and effective.

Developing systems for regular improvement assessment is where you turn that vigilant monitoring into actionable insights. Performance benchmarking is a powerful tool in this arsenal, allowing you to compare your operations against industry standards or competitors. It's like having a friendly competition that pushes you to improve continuously. Regular process audits also play a critical role here. By routinely evaluating your processes, you pinpoint inefficiencies and areas for enhancement. This practice keeps your operations lean and agile, ready to adapt to new challenges or opportunities. By integrating

89

these assessments into your routine, you create a culture of continuous improvement that permeates every level of your organization.

Technology is your ally in enhancing monitoring and improvement efforts. Automated monitoring systems act like a 24/7 surveillance team, keeping an eye on your operations and alerting you to potential issues before they become problems. These systems free up your team to focus on strategic initiatives rather than getting bogged down by routine checks. AI-driven process optimization tools take this a step further, using complex algorithms to identify patterns and suggest enhancements. Imagine having a digital assistant that not only flags issues but also proposes solutions, helping you optimize your processes continuously. By embracing technology, you streamline your monitoring efforts, making them more efficient and effective.

Industry best practices offer a treasure trove of insights for fostering continuous improvement. Lean Six Sigma methodologies, for example, provide a structured approach to process improvement, focusing on eliminating waste and enhancing quality. It's like having a playbook that guides you toward operational excellence. Kaizen, a Japanese philosophy of incremental improvement, encourages everyone in the organization to seek ways to enhance processes. By cultivating a Kaizen mindset, you empower your team to take ownership of improvements, fostering a culture where small, consistent changes lead to significant long-term benefits. These practices create an environment where continuous improvement is not just a goal but a way of life.

Building a Roadmap for Future Cost Management Success

Creating a roadmap for future cost management success is akin to plotting a course for a long journey, ensuring you reach your destination efficiently and effectively. The first step in this process involves setting long-term cost-saving goals. These goals act as your guiding lights, providing direction and purpose to your cost management efforts. Once you've established your objectives, identifying key milestones and deliverables becomes crucial. These markers serve as checkpoints along the way, helping you measure progress and make necessary adjustments. A well-crafted roadmap ensures that every member of your team is aligned with the organization's vision, working cohesively towards shared goals.

Incorporating flexibility and adaptability into your roadmap is essential for navigating the ever-changing business landscape. Scenario planning allows you to anticipate potential disruptions and prepare contingency plans, ensuring you remain agile and resilient. By considering various scenarios, you equip yourself with strategies to tackle unexpected challenges while seizing opportunities. Feedback mechanisms also play a vital role in this process, providing a channel for real-time insights and adjustments. By fostering an environment where feedback is valued and acted upon, you create a roadmap that's not only robust but also responsive to the needs of the organization.

Engaging stakeholders in the development of your roadmap is vital to its success. Collaborative planning sessions bring together diverse perspectives, fostering a sense of ownership and commitment among team members. By involving stakeholders in the decision-making process, you ensure that the roadmap reflects the collective wisdom and expertise of the organization. Stakeholder feedback integration is another key element, allowing you to refine your roadmap based on input from those directly impacted by its implementation. This collaborative approach not only enhances the roadmap's effectiveness but also strengthens the bonds within your team, creating a united front in the pursuit of cost management success.

Examples of effective cost management roadmaps abound in various industries, offering valuable lessons for those embarking on this journey. In the manufacturing sector, companies that have successfully implemented strategic roadmaps often emphasize the importance of aligning short-term actions with long-term goals. By maintaining focus on their ultimate objectives, these organizations navigate challenges with confidence, ensuring sustainable growth. In the service sector, businesses that prioritize customer feedback and adaptability in their roadmaps often achieve greater success in meeting evolving demands. By drawing inspiration from these examples, you can craft a roadmap that propels your organization toward future cost management success.

Building a Roadmap for Future Cost Management Success

Creating a roadmap for future cost management success is much like plotting a course for a long and rewarding journey. It requires careful planning and foresight. The first step involves setting long-term cost-saving goals. These goals serve as your guiding stars, providing direction and clarity on where you want your organization to be. When setting these goals, consider both the immediate savings you hope to achieve and the broader financial health of your organization. Once your goals are clear, identify key milestones and deliverables that will mark progress along the way. These milestones act like checkpoints, helping you measure success and stay on track. They provide tangible targets that your team can rally around, ensuring everyone is aligned and moving in the same direction.

Flexibility and adaptability are crucial elements to incorporate into your roadmap. Business conditions are ever-changing, and your roadmap should be able to evolve accordingly. Scenario planning plays a pivotal role here. By envisioning potential disruptions— whether economic shifts, technological advancements, or unexpected challenges—you prepare your organization to face them with confidence. It's about having a plan B, C, and D, ready to go when needed. Moreover, incorporating feedback mechanisms ensures that your roadmap remains dynamic and responsive to real-world conditions. Regularly gathering input from key stakeholders allows you to make informed adjustments, ensuring that your strategies remain relevant and effective. This adaptability is not just a safety net; it's a strategic advantage that keeps your organization agile and responsive to change.

Engaging stakeholders in the development of your roadmap is vital for its success. Collaborative planning sessions bring diverse perspectives to the table, fostering a sense of ownership and commitment among all involved. These sessions encourage open dialogue and idea-sharing, leading to more innovative and effective strategies. Stakeholder feedback integration is an essential component, ensuring that the roadmap reflects the collective insights and expertise of your team. By involving stakeholders from across the organization, you build a roadmap that is both comprehensive and well-rounded. This collaborative approach not only enhances the roadmap's quality but also ensures buy-in from those responsible for its execution, creating a united front in pursuit of cost management success.

Examples of effective cost management roadmaps abound, offering valuable lessons for those looking to forge their path. Consider a manufacturing company that successfully implemented a strategic roadmap focused on future growth. By setting ambitious yet achievable cost-saving goals, they were able to streamline operations and reduce waste significantly. Key milestones included the integration of advanced technologies and the optimization of supply chain processes, leading to substantial cost reductions. In the service sector, a company embarked on a roadmap that prioritized customer feedback and adaptability. By continuously refining their services based on customer insights, they achieved enhanced customer satisfaction and loyalty. These case studies illustrate that, regardless of industry, a well-crafted roadmap can guide organizations towards sustainable cost management success.

As we conclude this chapter, we've explored the importance of crafting a detailed and dynamic roadmap for cost management. By setting clear goals, embracing flexibility, engaging stakeholders, and learning from successful examples, you position your organization for long-term success. This roadmap is not just a plan on paper; it's a living document that guides your organization through the complexities of cost management, ensuring you remain competitive and resilient in a rapidly changing world.

NOTES:

Conclusion

As we come to the end of our journey through "The Profit Blueprint," let's take a moment to reflect on the key insights we've uncovered. Throughout this book, we've explored the critical role of strategic cost management in driving business success and resilience. We've seen how a comprehensive understanding of cost structures, coupled with innovative strategies and a cost-conscious culture, can transform organizations, enhancing efficiency and boosting profitability.

At the heart of this book lies a powerful message: cost management is not just about cutting expenses; it's about enabling sustainable growth and gaining a competitive edge. By aligning cost-saving initiatives with overall business objectives, you can create a synergistic effect that propels your organization forward. From optimizing supply chains to leveraging advanced financial techniques, the strategies we've discussed provide a roadmap for navigating the complex landscape of cost management.

As you reflect on the key takeaways from each chapter, consider how you can apply these insights to your own business context. Whether you're a financial manager looking to streamline budgeting processes or an entrepreneur seeking to optimize operational efficiency, the principles outlined in this book can guide your decision-making. Start by conducting a thorough analysis of your current cost structures, identifying areas where improvements can be made. Engage your team in this process, fostering a culture of cost-consciousness and continuous improvement.

Looking ahead, it's clear that the world of cost management is constantly evolving. As new technologies emerge and market dynamics shift, it's crucial to remain adaptable and open to innovative solutions. Embrace the power of data analytics, automation, and collaborative tools to stay ahead of the curve. By continuously seeking out best practices and staying attuned to industry trends, you can position your organization for long-term success.

On a personal note, writing this book has been an incredible journey for me. As someone who has worked in various industries and owned a business, I've seen firsthand the transformative power of effective cost management. My goal in sharing these insights is to empower you, the reader, to take control of your financial destiny and drive meaningful change within your organization. I hope that the strategies and examples provided in this book have sparked new ideas and inspired you to approach cost management with renewed energy and purpose.

As you embark on implementing these strategies, remember that you're not alone. I encourage you to share your experiences and insights with others, whether it's through professional networks, industry forums, or even reaching out to me directly. By engaging in dialogue and exchanging ideas, we can collectively elevate the practice of cost management and drive positive change across industries.

In the end, strategic cost management is not a destination but an ongoing journey. It requires commitment, adaptability, and a willingness to challenge the status quo. By embracing this mindset and leveraging the tools and techniques outlined in "The Profit Blueprint," you can unlock the full potential of your organization, driving profitability, efficiency, and long-term success.

So, my fellow cost management enthusiast, I invite you to take the insights from this book and run with them. Be bold in your approach, stay curious, and never stop seeking out new ways to optimize your business. The future belongs to those who can effectively navigate the complexities of cost management, and with the knowledge gained from this book, you're well on your way to mastering this critical skill.

Remember, every journey begins with a single step. Take that step today, and let "The Profit Blueprint" be your guide as you chart a course towards a more profitable and sustainable future. Together, we can redefine the landscape of cost management and build organizations that thrive in the face of any challenge.

References

- *Variable Cost vs. Fixed Cost: What's the Difference?* https://www.investopedia.com/ask/answers/032515/what-difference-between-variable-cost-and-fixed-cost-economics.asp#:~:text=Fixed%20costs%20are%20expenses%20that,%2C%20commissions%2C%20and%20raw%20materials.
- *The Impact of Cost Structure on Pricing Strategies* https://fastercapital.com/content/Business-cost-structure--The-Impact-of-Cost-Structure-on-Pricing-Strategies.html
- *Understanding Hidden Costs in Your Supply Chain* https://www.supplychainbrain.com/ext/resources/secure_download/KellysFiles/WhitePapersAndBenchMarkReports/Purolator/purolator_hidden_costs.pdf
- *Key Performance Indicators (kpis) For Cost Control* https://fastercapital.com/topics/key-performance-indicators-(kpis)-for-cost-control.html
- *Strategic Sourcing Best Practices: A Comprehensive List* https://www.netsuite.com/portal/resource/articles/erp/strategic-sourcing-best-practices.shtml
- *Lean Manufacturing Made Toyota Successful* https://www.mfg.marshall.edu/lean-manufacturing-made-toyota-the-success-story-it-is-today/
- *The Costs and Benefits of Hybrid Work* https://globalworkplaceanalytics.com/resources/costs-benefits
- *Cost Savings & Benefits of Cloud Computing* https://technologyadvice.com/blog/information-technology/4-ways-cloud-computing-can-save-money/
- *Zero-Based Budgeting (ZBB): A Guide for Business Leaders* https://www.gartner.com/smarterwithgartner/use-zero-based-budgeting-to-rightsize-tight-budgets
- *The Top 20 Best Cash Flow Management Software for ...* https://www.striven.com/the-top-20-best-cash-flow-management-software-for-small-business
- *21 best financial forecasting software solutions for 2025* https://www.cubesoftware.com/blog/financial-forecasting-software-tools

- *Cutting Costs: The Role of Risk Management in Cost ...* https://fastercapital.com/content/Cutting-Costs--The-Role-of-Risk-Management-in-Cost-Reduction.html
- *Principles Of Lean Supply Chain Management* https://tikalacademy.com/principles-of-lean-supply-chain-management
- *Maximizing cost savings through strategic sourcing - Amplio* https://www.getamplio.com/post/maximizing-cost-savings-through-strategic-sourcing
- *What Is a Transportation Management System?* https://www.oracle.com/scm/logistics/transportation-management/what-is-transportation-management-system/
- *The Best Inventory Management Software* https://www.pcmag.com/picks/the-best-inventory-management-software
- *Automation at scale: The benefits for payers* https://www.mckinsey.com/~/media/McKinsey/Industries/Healthcare%20Systems%20and%20Services/Our%20Insights/Automation%20at%20scale%20The%20benefits%20for%20payers/Automation-at-scale-The-benefits-for-payers.pdf
- *Achieving Cost Optimization through Data-Driven Strategies* https://www.zanovoy.com/blog-posts/achieving-cost-optimization-through-data-driven-strategies
- *Cost Savings & Benefits of Cloud Computing* https://technologyadvice.com/blog/information-technology/4-ways-cloud-computing-can-save-money/
- *Applying Agile Methods To Your Business* https://managementconsulted.com/agile-methods/
- *The Role of Employee Engagement in Cost Reduction* https://www.hcoinnovations.com/the-role-of-employee-engagement-in-cost-reduction/
- *How Does Employee Training And Development Improve ...* https://www.granta-automation.co.uk/news/how-does-employee-training-and-development-improve-operational-efficiency/#:~:text=Employee%20training%20and%20development%20can,contributions%20to%20the%20organisation's%20success.

- *Prosci's Top 10 Tactics for Managing Resistance to Change* https://www.prosci.com/blog/prosci-top-10-tactics-for-managing-resistance-to-change
- *Why you need a Corporate Travel Incentive Program? - ITILITE's* https://www.itilite.com/blog/corporate-travel-incentive-program/
- *Case Studies of Successful Cost Reduction* https://eoxs.com/new_blog/case-studies-of-successful-cost-reduction/
- *25 Detailed Cost Reduction Techniques for Your Businesses* https://quandarycg.com/how-to-cut-costs-while-increasing-efficiency-in-your-business/
- *5 Reasons Why Many Cost Reduction Initiatives Fail* https://cfo.university/library/article/5-reasons-why-many-cost-reduction-initiatives-fail-chisambara
- *Effective Cost Management in IT: Strategies for Success* https://www.jenlor.com/blog/effective-cost-management-in-it-strategies-for-success/
- *The Impact of Cost Reduction Strategies on Business ...* https://aithor.com/essay-examples/the-impact-of-cost-reduction-strategies-on-business-profitability-and-sustainability
- *Sustainable Cost Management: The Manufacturer's Guide ...* https://www.deskera.com/blog/sustainable-cost-management-guide-manufacturer-profitability/
- *Strategic Cost Transformation | Solvay Case Study* https://www.accenture.com/us-en/case-studies/strategy/solvays-formula-growth
- *How Technology is Changing Cost Management* https://navan.com/blog/cost-savings/how-technology-is-changing-cost-management

BONUS

How to be Cost Super Hero

Six Strategies to Reduce Operational Costs While Improving Efficiency Without Layoffs, Salary Reductions, or Damaging Relationships

By

Dr. Daniel R Coleman, DBA, MBA

CEO – C.E.S. LLC

CBW Publishing - USA

All Rights Reserved 2025

978-0-9823158-8-0

Forward:

In my experience, when company leaders discuss cutting costs, the immediate focus often turns to reducing headcount, lowering labor expenses, outsourcing business operations, or minimizing supply costs. While these are viable options, the potential savings may be counterbalanced by unforeseen expenses or the risk of damaging established relationships.

For whom is the book written?

- **Financial Managers**: These professionals meticulously oversee budgeting and financial planning to ensure optimal cost structures and healthy profit margins. They seek books that provide actionable strategies for expense management and strategic cost reduction to enhance their financial acumen and decision-making prowess.

- **C-Suite Executives**: CEOs, CFOs, and COOs focus on big-picture strategies that drive corporate profitability. They value insights into operational efficiency and profitability enhancement, looking for books that offer strategic solutions and visionary ideas to implement within their organizations.

- **Operations and Supply Chain Managers**: Tasked with the nuts and bolts of procurement and logistics, these managers prioritize efficiency and cost optimization in the supply chain. Your book promises them valuable methodologies for streamlining operations and cutting excess costs in manufacturing and logistics.

- **Entrepreneurs and Business Owners**: These individuals juggle the complexities of scaling their businesses while maintaining profitability. They eagerly search for comprehensive guides on cost-saving strategies and budget optimization to sustain growth without sacrificing financial health.

Each of the following chapters introduces viable cost-saving programs that are either budget-neutral for the company to implement or offer a tangible ROI (Business Process Automation). In the case of Accounts Payable Automation, our partner provides a revenue stream while decreasing operational expenses.

Our consulting business matches companies with our partners who have proven their worth and can predict, with a reasonable amount of certainty, how much they can save your company. Each of our partners meets with potential clients for no up-front cost or fee. If you are looking for innovative and cutting-edge ways to lower your operational costs and improve your bottom line, this is a good place to start.

TABLE OF CONTENTS

INTRODUCTION – How to Become a Cost Super Hero

To stay competitive, every business must contend with the profit equation: Total Revenue – Total Costs = Profit. In my experience, every company executive and business owner is keenly focused on the challenge of increasing revenue. Michael Porter (1980) provided that one of three ways to achieve long-term profitability is to be a cost leader. Not a price leader, but a cost leader. If cutting costs brings to mind the need for employee layoffs, salary cuts, or quality reductions, the whole idea might put a bad taste in your mouth. The nightmare of disgruntled employees or chippy suppliers or unhappy customers is unsettling. Here are some of the challenges that come with the idea of cutting costs to establish yourself as a Cost Super Hero.

Challenges of Cutting Costs

- **Difficulty in Identifying Cost-Saving Opportunities**: Many financial managers struggle to pinpoint precise areas where costs can be reduced without negatively impacting operations. They often face this challenge while analyzing complex financial statements and reports, leading to missed opportunities for savings.

- **Balancing Cost Control with Quality**: C-suite executives frequently grapple with maintaining product or service quality while implementing cost-cutting measures. This dilemma often arises during

104

budget discussions where reducing expenses clashes with sustaining high standards.

- **Inefficient Supply Chain Processes**: Operations and supply chain managers often encounter inefficiencies in procurement and logistics, causing increased operational costs. These issues may stem from outdated processes or lack of integration between departments, resulting in delays and higher expenses.

- **Scaling Challenges for Entrepreneurs**: Entrepreneurs aiming to scale their businesses often find it hard to manage escalating costs while maintaining profitability. As their operations grow, they may struggle to keep a balance between expansion and cost efficiency.

- **Lack of Cross-Departmental Coordination**: Achieving cost control requires collaboration across different departments. Financial managers and operations executives often face silos within organizations, leading to duplicated efforts and missed cost-saving opportunities.

- **Overwhelming Data and Insufficient Analysis Tools**: With the abundance of data available, financial managers may find it overwhelming to analyze effectively without the right tools. This can result in inaccurate forecasts and ineffective cost-reduction strategies.

- **Resistance to Change**: Implementing new cost-saving strategies often meets resistance from employees accustomed to established procedures. This cultural hurdle can slow down or even derail cost optimization initiatives.

- **Inadequate Budget Optimization Techniques**: Many businesses lack sophisticated tools or methodologies for effective budget optimization, leading to suboptimal allocation of resources and financial inefficiencies.

- **Difficulty in Measuring Impact**: Businesses often struggle to measure the impact of cost-saving initiatives effectively. Without clear metrics and Key Performance Indicators (KPI) they find it challenging to assess the success of their strategies and make informed adjustments.

In the Lean Business Institute (a CES LLC initiative) book, *"The Profit Blueprint": Proven Strategies for Reducing Costs, Enhancing Efficiency, and Boosting Your Bottom-Line,* the process of transforming a business into a lean company follows a more prescriptive approach to the overall operations of a company. This book is intended to give you some immediate wins that don't require a lot of political capital or consensus. The following chapters cover at least one area that will apply to your business regardless of its industry, size, or competitive situation.

Note: Not all our partner programs are covered (Class Action Enrollment and Documentation; Tax Advocate Monitoring; Recouping Medical Underpayments from Insurance Providers, Tribal Tax Credits, Debt Resolution as an Employee Benefit), but if you would like more information, please contact us.

512-846-3175

www.cesbusinessadvisors.com
drc@cesbusinessadvisors.com

CHAPTER ONE

Commercial Payments - Turn your Accounts Payable Department into a Profit Center

In any business, where every dollar counts and relationships with suppliers are vital, the efficiency of financial operations can make or break an organization. As businesses continue to navigate complex financial landscapes, automation of the invoice-to-pay process emerges as a strategic tool that offers significant advantages.

1. Goal - Enhancing Working Capital

One of the most impactful benefits of automating the invoice-to-pay lifecycle is the improvement of working capital. By leveraging automation, healthcare organizations can free up cash that is often tied up in manual processes. This is achieved through mechanisms like generating rebates on card spend, capturing early payment discounts, and optimizing payment terms. Moreover, supply chain finance solutions can speed up supplier payments without negatively impacting the organization's balance sheet, providing a win-win situation for both the company and its suppliers.

Research Insight: Deloitte's (n.d.) research indicates that effective working capital management can lead to a substantial increase in liquidity, which is crucial for all companies that need to reinvest in other critical areas.

2. Goal - Strengthening Supplier Relationships

Strong supplier relationships are essential for the smooth operation of healthcare facilities. Automation helps by providing suppliers with multiple payment options, real-time visibility into the status of their payments, and the detailed remittance data they need. These features reduce the risk of supply chain disruptions caused by late payments and ensure a more reliable and responsive supply chain.

Research Insight: According to McKinsey (2022), a vast majority of suppliers value transparency and flexibility in payment processes, which significantly influences their willingness to maintain long-term partnerships.

3. Goal - Reducing Fraud Risks

In an era where payment fraud is increasingly sophisticated, automation can play a crucial role in protecting all types of organizations. Automated systems offer built-in permissions, business rules, real-time tracking, and secure payment methods to mitigate risks such as Business Email Compromise (BEC) attacks and phishing schemes.

Research Insight: A report by the Association for Financial Professionals (AFP) found that 81% of organizations experienced attempted or actual payment fraud in 2022, highlighting the critical need for secure, automated financial processes.

Solution– Turning Your Accounts Payable Department Into a Profit Center

What if you could monetize the accounts payable process from invoice receipt through payment reconciliation? Across the US and Europe, organizations like yours are achieving significant strategic benefits by automating their invoice-to-pay life cycle.

AP Automation has helped thousands of companies – AT NO COST TO THEM – generate significant efficiencies and turn their Accounts Payable department from a cost into a profit center.

1. **Working capital improvements** enable firms to free up cash on existing revenues by generating significant rebates on card spending, capturing more early payment discounts, and rationalizing their payment terms. They even offer a supply chain finance solution that speeds supplier payments without impacting your balance sheet.

2. **Stronger supplier relationships.** AP Automation strengthens supplier relationships by providing suppliers with options for how they get paid, real-time visibility into the status of their payments, and the rich remittance data they need to easily post your payments. There's also less chance of supply chain issues caused by late payments. Industry-leading vendor enablement services ensure you achieve optimal adoption of electronic payments –meaning more opportunities to earn card rebates, reduce costs, and mitigate risk.

3. **Less risk of fraud.** From Business Email Compromise attacks to phishing schemes, the risk of payment fraud is at an all-time high. AP Automation mitigates your risk of fraud with built-in permissions, business rules and controls, real-time tracking, and secure payment methods.

4. **Improved efficiency** is helping organizations reduce their cost to process supplier invoices and make payments to suppliers by 60 percent or more. That's money that your organizations can reinvest in their business or patient care.

5. There should be **no need to change banks** to make payments. Integration with many of the leading financial institutions in the United States, will allow you to automatically reconcile bank statements and close the books faster at the end of the month.

6. **ERP Integration.** Our CES Partner integrates with over 350 Enterprise Resource Planning (ERPs) and accounting software packages. Their connectivity extends the value of your ERP investments by automating reconciliation, improving cash flow and spend reporting, speeding the financial close, and, in some cases, making it possible to initiate payments from directly within your ERP.

CES, LLC has partnered with an industry-leading company that offers a bonafide, budget-neutral way to decrease costs and provide a revenue stream. Contact us for an introduction.

CASE STUDY

Property Management Company: A Detailed Overview

The property management industry is a significant sector in the real estate market, managing a diverse range of assets, from residential to commercial properties. This article delves into the structure of the property management industry, highlighting key market segments, target profiles, and the value propositions that drive business within this vertical.

Market Segmentation

The property management industry in the United States is extensive, with approximately 30,000 property management companies operating nationwide. These companies vary in size and scope, from small to mid-sized enterprises to large national firms. Understanding the breakdown of these segments provides insight into how the industry operates and the key players involved.

- HOA/Condo Management:

    o Nationwide Presence: There are about 9,000 management companies that focus on homeowners' associations (HOAs) and condominiums across the country.

    o Market Composition: Small to mid-sized companies dominate this segment, representing 84% of the total addressable market (TAM). These companies typically manage assets with average total accounts payable (A/P) of $50-90 million, with $6-10 million in card transactions

Multi/Single Family Management:

- Nationwide Presence: This segment consists of approximately 30,000 property management companies.

- Market Composition: Mid-to-large-sized companies make up 78% of this industry. They handle assets with an average total A/P ranging from $40-100 million, with $5-12 million managed through card transactions.

- ERP Systems: Key enterprise resource planning (ERP) systems used in this segment include Yardi, AppFolio, and Rent Manager

Target Profiles in Property Management

For companies targeting the property management sector, understanding the profiles of potential clients is crucial. These target profiles include:

- Owners/Presidents and CFOs:

  o These individuals are the primary decision-makers in property management companies.

  o They are often interested in solutions that can manage a spend target of $350,000 per month or greater, making them ideal candidates for rebate programs and financial management tools.

- Property Management Companies:

    o The focus is on companies managing large-scale properties, including HOA/Condo/Co-op, multi/single family units, and manufactured homes.

    o Commercial/retail and office properties also represent a significant portion of the target market

Value Propositions for Property Management Companies

Our CES Partner offers compelling value propositions that address the industry's unique needs. Some of the key value propositions include:

- Transparency and Digital Workflow:

    o Solutions that provide transparency in financial transactions and streamline digital workflows for boards of directors (BOD) and managers are highly valued.

- Increased Operational Efficiencies:

    o Enhance operational efficiencies, reducing the time and cost associated with managing large portfolios.

- Fraud Reduction and Payment Transparency:

- - With large sums of money being managed, fraud reduction and transparent payment processes are critical concerns for these companies.

- New Revenue Sources:

  - Innovative solutions that create additional revenue streams are attractive, particularly in a competitive market.

Accounts Payable Rebate Program

Property Management Overview

HOA/Condo

- 9,000 Management companies nationwide
- Small to Mid-size companies represent 85% of the TAM
- **Average Total A/P:** $50-75M ~ $0.5-10M card
- Larger National companies: 15% of the market
- **Average Total A/P:** $100-500M ~ $13-16M card
- **ERPs:** VMS, FrontSteps, Vantaca

Multi/Single Family

- 30,000 property management companies nationwide
- Mid to Large companies represent 75% of the industry
- **Average Total A/P:** $50-75M ~ $1-2M in card
- Mixed assets; Own & Manage only
- **ERPs:** Yardi, AppFolio, Rent Manager

Commercial/Retail/Office

- 3,200 Management companies
- 85% of the industry is Small to Mid-size, and represent largest % of S+S, footprint
- 20% of industry assets are owned by larger companies
- **Larger companies:** NAi-Cushman/Wakefield+JLL

- **ERPs:** Yardi, MRI, AppFolio, MDS

Conclusion

The property management industry is a complex and diverse sector, with significant opportunities for companies that understand the nuances of the market. By targeting the right profiles and offering tailored value propositions, service providers can position themselves as key partners in this dynamic industry.

CASE STUDY

Hospitality Industry

Total Opportunity

- $60 Billion: The total accounts payable (AP) opportunity in the hospitality industry.

- $580 Million+: Currently captured through virtual card solutions.

- 1,100+: Potential management organizations within the industry.

- 90+ Active Organizations: Representing over 1,200 hotels.

Hospitality Market Overview

The U.S. hospitality industry generates $197 billion in revenue from over 30,000 hotels.

Key characteristics:

- Virtual card market share currently stands at 4%.

- The market has stabilized post-pandemic, with 2023 revenue levels reaching those of 2019.

- Financial pressures from rising wages and interest rates are driving the need for efficiency.

Leading Brands:

- Four Seasons, Montage, Loews, Fairmont, Sonesta.

Hotel Segmentation

Hotel Tiers:

- Economy/Midscale: Budget-friendly options.

- Select Service/Upscale: Some full-service amenities.

- Upper Upscale/Luxury: Primarily full-service properties.

- Destination/Lifestyle/Boutique: Unique experiences in targeted locales.

Hotel Ownership and Operations

Ownership Structures:

1. Independent Investors.

2. Ownership Investment Groups.

3. Private Equity/REITs (Non-Operators).

Operational Organizations:

- Private Management Companies: Responsible for operations and financial performance, including hiring, sales, guest satisfaction, revenue management, brand compliance, and profitability.

- National Brands: Oversee multi-property portfolios and brand adherence.

Asset Structures:

- May include multi-asset, multi-treasury, and mixed-management portfolios.

- Management organizations may hold equity positions or provide third-party services.

- Accounting systems may be centralized (corporate office) or decentralized (property-specific).

Target Profiles

Key decision-makers and profiles for solutions in the hospitality vertical:

- Roles: CFOs, VPs of Accounting, VPs of Procurement.

- Portfolios: Minimum of 15+ hotels.

- Revenue Size: At least $35 million annually.

- Monthly Spend Targets: $750,000 or greater.

Industry Insights

Asset Mixes:

- Portfolios often include a mix of branded select-service and luxury hotels (e.g., Marriott, Hilton, Hyatt, IHG).

- Destination and boutique properties are also common, though generally smaller in size.

Target Portfolios to Avoid:

- Casinos and international portfolios.

Value Propositions

Solutions aimed at addressing hospitality needs focus on:

1. Fraud Reduction across multi-entity/multi-treasury structures.

2. Supplier Relationships: Timely payments to maintain strong vendor connections.

3. Invoice Automation & Vendor Management: Streamlining accounts payable processes.

4. Automated Reconciliation: Reducing manual labor and errors.

5. Resource Efficiencies: Enhancing operational and financial efficiency.

Conclusion

The hospitality industry represents a significant opportunity for innovation and efficiency, with $60 billion in total accounts payable potential and a growing interest in virtual payment solutions. Despite market stabilization post-pandemic, rising operational costs and financial pressures are driving the need for streamlined processes and resource optimization.

Targeting portfolios with a minimum of 15 hotels and annual revenues of $35 million or more, key decision-makers such as CFOs and VPs of Procurement prioritize solutions that address fraud reduction, timely supplier payments, and automated reconciliation. By focusing on branded select-service and luxury portfolios, alongside boutique and destination properties, the industry is well-positioned for value-driven solutions that enhance financial performance and operational efficiency.

This case study underscores the potential for strategic innovation within the hospitality sector to drive profitability, improve vendor relationships, and streamline financial processes.

CASE STUDY

Golf Resort and Country Clubs

Industry: Hospitality and Leisure

The Challenge:

Golf resorts and country clubs face unique operational challenges, including:

1. Talent Management:

   o Difficulty attracting and retaining qualified staff in a competitive market.

2. Operational Efficiency:

- o Ownership mandates to "do more with less," often stretching resources thin.

3. Financial Fraud Risks:

   - o An increase in check fraud incidents and other financial vulnerabilities.

4. Expense and Cash Management:

   - o Higher expectations for precision in managing expenses and cash flow.

The Solution

Our CES Partner introduced a comprehensive Commercial Payments strategy to tackle these issues:

Accounts Payable (AP) Automation

- Transitioned nearly 50% of vendors to CSI Pay systems, reducing reliance on traditional payment methods.

- Eliminated manual check production through AP automation, saving time and minimizing risk.

Enhanced Cash Flow Management

- Implemented advanced invoice automation technologies capable of processing over $100 billion in annual invoice spend.

- Automated workflows to minimize human operator intervention, enhancing accuracy and speed.

Integrated Systems for Efficiency

- Combined payment, invoicing, and expense management into a seamless solution integrated with existing ERPs and accounting systems.

The Results

BPA adoption resulted in significant improvements:

1. Cost Savings:

   o Eliminated check-related costs, saving $4,217 annually.

   o Generated $1,500 in monthly rebates for participating clubs.

   o Total annual return of $21,893, with a projected 5-year return of $109,462.

2. Time Efficiency:

   o Simplified the payables process to mere minutes, freeing staff for higher-value activities.

3. Improved Risk Management:

   o Reduced financial fraud risks through enhanced security measures.

4. Enhanced Vendor Relationships:

   o Improved payment processes strengthened trust and collaboration with vendors.

Why Commercial Payments Automation (CPA) Matters

For golf and country clubs, operational challenges often limit growth and efficiency. CPA provides a pathway to:

- Simplify complex processes.

- Reduce operational costs.

- Strengthen financial security.

- Enhance service quality for members and stakeholders.

How to Become a Cost Super Hero is available on Amazon.

Amazon.com: HOW TO BECOME A COST SUPERHERO: Six Strategies to Reduce Operational Costs While Improving Efficiency Without Layoffs, Salary Reductions, or Damaging ... Costs - The Fastest Way to Increase Profits): 9780982315880: Coleman DBA, Daniel R., Coleman DBA, Dr. Daniel R: Books